The Other 23 & a Half Hours

BOOKS BY CATHERINE OWEN

*Catalysts: Confrontations with the muse*
*Cusp/detritus: An experiment in alleyways*
*Dark Fish & Other Infernos*
*Designated Mourner*
*Dog*
*Frenzy*
*Seeing Lessons*
*Shall: ghazals*
*Somatic: The life and work of Egon Schiele*
*Trobairitz*
*The Wrecks of Eden*

# The Other 23 & a Half Hours

## Or Everything You Wanted to Know that Your MFA Didn't Teach You

### CATHERINE OWEN

WOLSAK
& WYNN

Cover and interior design: Marijke Friesen
Author's photograph: Catherine Owen
Typeset in Dante
Printed by Coach House Printing Company Toronto, Canada

The publisher gratefully acknowledges the support of the Canada Council for the Arts, the Ontario Arts Council and the Canada Book Fund.

Wolsak and Wynn Publishers Ltd.
280 James Street North
Hamilton, ON
Canada L8R 2L3

Library and Archives Canada Cataloguing in Publication

Owen, Catherine, 1971–, author
    The other 23 & a half hours, or, Everything you wanted to know that your M.F.A. didn't teach you / Catherine Owen.

Includes bibliographical references.
ISBN 978-1-928088-00-4 (paperback)

1. Authorship. 2. Criticism—Canada. I. Title. II. Title: Other twenty-three and a half hours. III. Title: Everything you wanted to know that your M.F.A. didn't teach you.

PN145.O94 2015          808.02          C2015-903288-1

# Table of Contents

# Introduction

*The hardest thing about being a poet [is] knowing what to do with the other 23 and a half hours of the day.*
– Max Beerbohm as recollected by Billy Collins, "Words, Words, Words"

*Poetry is a way of life.*
– Robin Skelton, *The Practice of Poetry*

When I first started writing I was very young, about four or five years old. I had no idea of what a writer did but write. And, of course, read. Even by the time I was in my late teens and giving my early poetry readings, my vision of the writer's life was confined to the romantic image of the poet ensconced in their garret. That poet was interested only in churning out the next poem, perhaps submitting it to a magazine or press in hope of publication, and undertaking readings, which seemed to be required for a poet in the twentieth century. It wasn't until my mid-twenties that I really started to enlarge my vision of what living the life of a writer or a poet means.

Of course, the writing is paramount, publishing is essential and recitation is vital, but these are not the only pacts you make with your art when you assume the strange mantle of a poet in North America. Our business-driven, almost wholly prosaic society attempts to convince all of us that creating art doesn't matter, that it's irrelevant and that the poet has little contribution to make. Or, as with the general mandate of M.F.A. programs, like the one I briefly attended in the summer of 2011, that writing poems is bound up in a source of employment and prestige. The underlying message is that composing poetry leads to a teaching career and that to obtain and keep that job one must "publish or perish" along with other academics. Such an expectation can frustrate artists in many ways. It can convince them to stop writing and detach them from the possibility they can make an impact on the world, or limit their work to acts that lead only to professional ends. More often than not, poets are told that the only way they can use their talents beyond writing itself is by teaching others. Important as this career path may be, there is a vast array of additional options for the poet who wishes to expand the boundaries of their art, contribute to their community and experiment with the fusion of genres and mediums to imagine whole new artistic visions.

The books that most poets and writers tend to read about their artistic practice concern themselves with the act of writing and getting it published. They have titles like *Writing Poetry, The Practice of Poetry, The Poet's Companion* and *Some Instructions on Writing & Life*. These guides all contain writing exercises and marketing tips. As useful as such texts are, *The Other 23 & a Half Hours* sets out to present a very different type of book. Over the last fifteen years or so, I have engaged in a range of artistic practices beyond writing itself. I have memorized poems, spent extensive time on scholarly research and written reviews of my contemporaries' publications; I have run two small chapbook presses and co- or solo hosted a half dozen performance series; I have worked with musicians, photographers and multimedia artists both alongside and outside the poem; I have held slightly weird jobs such as ad salesperson for a tattoo magazine and production assistant in film and TV; and I have travelled to parts of Europe, Mexico and the Middle East with the aim of learning about art from other cultures. A while ago, I began to ask myself, why have I done all these things? What have they contributed to my art and to the artistic community itself? Why do I feel these ways of being in the world are so important?

Armed with these questions, I began to pay attention to what other Canadian poets were doing in the community, noticing in the process the extensive range of activities many are involved in. Thus, I decided, over the course of several years, to interview fifty-eight Canadian poets on these practices, adding others I haven't undertaken myself to any serious extent, such as translation and running a radio show. I wanted to know what they did to make poetry matter in the world, whether they allied themselves with the university or the "streets," regardless of whether they self-identify as lyric or language poets, surrealists or formalists. As I spoke to the poetic community, I was filled with awe at how much we are all undertaking, often for very little remuneration or attention, to imbue the art with energy and a diversity of engagement. *The Other 23 & a Half Hours* is not a teaching text. It lays out no program, presents no assignments that will lead to grades, promises no path that proffers a potential job and prestige. Instead, this compendium is a journey of sorts through the experiences poets have as they go about making their art and seeing what can happen to it when they maintain an eternally questing mind and a generous dollop of attention.

Whether you call yourself a poet or a writer, are just beginning to write or have already published a book, have a full-time job and family or have chosen to be entirely committed to the writing life, *The Other 23 & a Half Hours* wants you to know there's more to writing than just writing, that you can be part of an energetic, demanding and fun as hell community of people who want to make poetry matter beyond the page. Get ready for a blast of truly rewarding "sweat equity."

# School or the Streets?: The M.F.A. versus the World Debate

*The Other 23 & a Half Hours* is subtitled *Or Everything You Wanted to Know that Your M.F.A. Didn't Teach You.* Where am I going with this? Am I suggesting M.F.A.s are unnecessary or perhaps even harmful approaches to writing? And that this book is a more apropos mode of learning things about writers and their community because it's random, encompassing (though not completist) and exists outside academic criteria? No, not entirely. The subtitle is, in part, a serious critique of what can be missed out on if one chooses to focus solely on getting writing degrees, then submerging oneself in the academic milieu; the perils of making writing "inseparable from its institutional context," as paraphrased by Chad Harbach in *n+1*, and part a poke at the notion that any one source, whether a degree or this book, will instruct you in everything you need to learn as a poet. As Donald Hall stresses, "All coterie associations . . . limit the possibilities of change and growth."

Taking my own history as a case in point (though can it ever be?), I started writing at around four years old just after I learned to read and wrote avidly throughout my childhood and adolescence in whatever genre appealed. At sixteen, I dropped out of school. Returning to complete a bachelor's and master's in English literature by the time I was thirty, I eschewed creative writing programs of any kind, feeling they would impose a shape on my writing routine and sources that would seem inorganic to me, while allowing myself to take the occasional workshop: with Patrick Lane in Sechelt, BC, over the course of four days in 1993; another time, in 2005, through the tutelage of George Elliott Clarke for ten days at the renowned Sage Hill Writing Experience in Saskatoon, SK.

Workshops, unlike academic writing programs, usually only last a brief time, from several hours to a few weeks, and often allow the "student" to apprentice under a writer they admire, enabling them to learn more readily from their experiences and perspectives rather than from a textbook or exercises. Most of the writers I interacted with – from my ex-husband Chad Norman to Al Purdy, Phyllis Webb, Ernest Hekkanen, Jamie Reid, Dennis E. Bolen, Goh Poh Seng, Joanne Arnott and so forth – seemed to have more iconoclastic modes of composition and of earning a living too. My goal was to write as much as possible while obtaining a paycheque in almost whatever way I could.

Starting in 1998, I began publishing trade books of poetry. My method of approach to poems was often research based but free, I felt, of any confines relating to "publish or perish" or "produce to please." Then, in 2011, after my spouse died unexpectedly, I suddenly felt fear clench me. I was getting older, rapidly, it seemed. How would I survive as a poet in the future? This anxiety propelled me toward the M.F.A. program at the University of British Columbia (UBC). I attended, as mentioned, for ten days, the creative nonfiction course, during July. And I was struck, first, by the fact that not only did several of the instructors not have M.F.A. degrees, but had been hired (as one should be) on the basis of their writing, not their academic achievements, and second, how most of my classmates had published little and appeared to be doing a degree to achieve greater compositional discipline and, yes, to get a job. Panel discussions revolved around what journals to publish in, how to compose a cover letter and tips for dealing with post-M.F.A. terror. Although I appreciated some of the commentary on my personal essay, I realized within a few days that this was not my world and I would have to seek survival elsewhere. In the M.F.A. program I felt as if I was backpedalling and discounting all I had learned up to that point by simply writing and living and trying to make community with other artists.

*The Other 23 & a Half Hours* began here. I know M.F.A. degrees work beautifully for some poets by offering them the chance to influence other writers and make a living in the process but I still question their motives, their results, but mostly, their hegemony. Certainly, getting an M.F.A. is not the only way to live in the world as a poet.

Historically speaking, M.F.A. programs haven't been around that long. The first course in creative writing was offered at the University of Iowa in 1895. Then, in 1936, Iowa launched the Writers' Workshop and began awarding the first M.F.A.s, according to Louis

Menand in an article for *The New Yorker* called "Show or Tell: Should Creative Writing be Taught?" Post-WWII there was a sudden upsurge in demand for university programs in every subject, including the arts, and the creative writing field burgeoned from this movement toward professionalization. In the US more than in Canada (whose first M.F.A. program wasn't launched until 1965 by Earle Birney at UBC), and particularly over the past decade or so, M.F.A. programs have come under critique. One reason for this may be their incredible growth. As Chad Harbach points out in "MFA vs NYC," there were "79 degree-granting programs in creative writing in 1975; today there are 854!" Pearl Luke's website, *Be a Better Writer*, lists seventeen universities offering M.F.A.s in Canada and the numbers are swelling, with some institutions like the University of Calgary even offering a Ph.D. in creative writing. Mark McGurl's *The Program Era: Postwar Fiction and the Rise of Creative Writing*, which focuses more on fiction than poetry in terms of the postwar proliferation of university writing programs, discusses some of the other reasons this may be the case.

The root issue is money, of course; who makes it, who truly benefits from these programs and, extending these questions, how, as McGurl notes, "the more important financial relationship between writers and the academy is about *teaching* creative writing, not studying it." In other words, the aim is to equip writers with connections that enable them to publish and thus, by adding to their academic credentials, to obtain sources of employment. It is not to educate students on how to read per se; on the difficult, mysterious craft of composition or other aspects that lie outside what can be taught, especially by an often ill-equipped workshopping group led only provisionally by an instructor. Graduate writing degrees may also change how the author views publishing. Harbach states that, in relation to fiction at least, "for the MFA writer, then, publishing a book becomes not a primary way to earn money or even a direct *attempt* to make money. The book instead serves as a credential." While poets rarely produce books hoping to make money, the creation of a collection should still be so much more crucial than adding to one's credentials. The bigger issue, as reviewer Carolyn Kellogg addresses, is whether, "institutionalizing a creative endeavor benefits our culture" (quoted in Jamison).

One of the most vociferous critics of the M.F.A.-dominant system is Raymond P. Hammond, whose book, *Poetic Amusement*, launches a relentless attack on poets who "professionalize," claiming that university courses in writing exist to "demystify" the art, in the process ousting the muse, glutting the publishing market with mediocrity and putting pressure on poets to produce simply to get and keep jobs rather than due to essential internal dictates. Poetry should be written, Hammond asserts, from a sense of tradition and poetic stewardship, as well as personal obsession, not from superficial contemporaneity, a desire to "get ahead in the game" and external "prompts."

Of course, nothing is ever a simple dichotomy. Very few writers are wholly a creation of either school or the streets. The poets in this book range from an esteemed anthologist and professor in creative writing, Gary Geddes, to a liminal writer without degrees at all, Mark McCawley; from a former office worker, Sandy Shreve, to a rancher, Garry Gottfriedson, to a psychiatrist, Ron Charach, and almost everything in between. Yet, our society is inevitably moving toward an emphasis on credentialization for almost all jobs, with even the manager of a waffle house, as Carl L. Bankston III pointed out in a 2011 article called "Adrift or Foundering?" being required to hold a degree in this day and age.

As Leslie Jamison underlines, "cultures are heavily cross-bred, and . . . each of these distinct 'cultures' is in fact composed of multiple forms of attachment to a single economic engine (the university or the publishing industry)," while Harbach determines that "it's time to do away with this distinction between the MFAs and the non-MFAs, the unfree and the free, the caged and the wild." Thus, within whichever kind of constraints, academic or "the streets," there remains a whole host of practices that encourage the writer to value, celebrate, transform and articulate what it means to create in the largest sense, beyond attention to end results or the final return on one's "investment."

# Reading, Revising and Performing

*You run into people who want to write poetry who don't want to read any-thing in the tradition. That's like wanting to be a builder but not finding out what different kinds of wood you use.*
– Gary Snyder, "The Real Work (excerpts from an interview)"

Reading is an act of love for language and books are our most crucial teachers. Back in the old days – that is, the '70s – people, if they provided poetry at all to children, didn't just stick to Shel Silverstein and Dennis Lee. My parents bought me my first poetry anthology when I was three years old. A weighty tome full of garish illustra-tions, it nonetheless featured poems by Emily Dickinson, Langston Hughes and Lord Byron, among many other demigods in the literary pantheon. For ages, I confused the drawing of a frog with the author of "I'm Nobody! Who are You?," but perhaps that can be forgiven in a preschooler. Every Saturday, my mother took her brood to the public library and we picked out twenty-five books for the week. And at school I could often be found in a corner bracketed by towers of reading material. Eventually, my selection veered away from *Anne of Green Gables* and toward *Wifey* by the notorious Judy Blume, and my taste in poems from William Butler Yeats' "Lake Isle of Innisfree" to Mötley Crüe lyrics. (Okay, okay, so it's not poetry, but it had a definite aural and sensorial impact on me then.)

By the time I was in my late teens, though, I was poetry-hungry again and lived in the section of the library that held Anne Sexton, Ted Hughes and P. K. Page. I was convinced if I devoured every single title, then, at the end, I would be able to write a good poem. Definitely not a shortcut. And the better poems only came after much reading, then scrawling and discarding. Without devouring so many words, there is no way I could have trained my ear and eye to what works, becoming, as I read, both more passionate and more critical about language. Steven Heighton, a writer living in Kingston, jots down thoughts to himself on reading in his short guide called *Workbook: Memos & Dispatches on Writing*. One of these is: "Reading great prose or poetry is like undergoing corrective laser surgery: it sears away the cataracts of habit." Vancouver spoken word artist Chris Gilpin uses another metaphor, equating the need for poets to read before and as they write with the need for "athletes to devour carbohydrates prior to a marathon." Quite simply, reading gives poets energy to create, it nourishes the core of their art and it enables them to endure as artists. Books are the poet's first and finest guides and mentors. Some poets will claim that they don't read much because they are afraid of being influenced. This argument has always seemed ridiculous to me.

First of all, we are the culmination of our influences and the more you read, the more you can develop a unique approach to your art. Secondly, if you don't read, you have little sense of history, theory, stylistic methodologies or perspectives to draw from. This knowledge serves as the material from which your poems are shaped. Others will say they don't have the money or time to purchase or read books. And my response is, if you have no time to read, please don't find the time to write. Reading comes first. It can be slipped into many areas of your life, from the time you commute on the bus to the moments you sit in the bath. And there are always libraries, free book bins, book sharing among friends. Books can also be ordered at low prices on sites like AbeBooks.com. One can even download public domain books for free into an e-reader from sites like Project Gutenberg. However, if you want readers to buy your books, I believe you must be willing to purchase other people's texts. Writing is the least expensive of all the art forms and yes, at times, it seems to be the art form that makes the least money, but books truly aren't very pricey and they give back far more than they take. Most importantly, books are our deepest companions.

# Revision

*In working on a poem, I love to revise. Lots of younger poets don't enjoy this, but in the process of revision I discover things.*
– Rita Dove, "Brushed by an Angel's Wings"

Reading comes first, then writing, then where does one go? Many writing guides provide exercises to stimulate the act of creation and then offer ideas on where to market the poems that emerge. Few remind the emerging poet that revision is a crucial part of writing. Revising a poem *can* feel like a process of discovery where the poet comes to understand why certain words or line breaks or images aren't effective in the particular piece. The poet must then experiment with other options in diction and form until the poem sounds right to the ear and the mind. At times, editing a poem offers a series of epiphanies; at others, it just seems a futile struggle that takes the poem further and further away from completion. While "first thought, best thought" was the mantra of Allen Ginsberg and many other Modernists, few recall that it was only a long-term-meditation practice and an immense amount of reading that turned Ginsberg into a reliable channel for words that seemingly came unbidden. Even if a poem seems to surge out magically, usually at least a few words require tweaking or torqueing. And once the poems have grown into a book-length manuscript, they will almost always demand restructuring to fit the emerging flow of the book in terms of its narrative and musical pacing.

In a blog for the *Ottawa Poetry Newsletter*, poet Peter Norman insists that "the bulk of poetry composition is editing. You write a poem once, but you rewrite or edit it up to hundreds of times. That initial surge of inspiration and excitement is important. But if it's true that execution rather than content determines a poem's quality, then it's those obsessive hours of subsequent swabbing and polishing that make or break the poem." Adam Dickinson from St. Catharines elaborates: "Editing for me is often where the art begins. There is a great deal of pleasure involved for me with massaging a text, playing around with it, making it stretch in different ways." Edmontonian Alice Major concurs, enlarging on this necessary process by noting that her "favourite part of writing poetry is revising. It is in the smoothing and fitting and finishing that the pleasure of craft really comes in." She has "two overall priorities in revising. First, sanding each line to a high gloss – making sure that rhythm and sound really work. Second is making the drawers slide smoothly for the users. Can readers get what I am trying to communicate? Is it actually saying anything interesting? I am of the school that feels the main purpose of poetry *is* communication."

I can't help but agree. While I truly believe there are poems roiling around in me that emerge almost perfect, many other pieces require structural and word-based editing, immediately and over a certain period of time after the initial draft. Once your book is accepted for publication, however, and has gone through multiple edits, then it's time to let go. The risk has been assumed and the work now needs to be released into the world.

# Performing

*The poetry reading is a public tuning.*
– Charles Bernstein, *My Way*

Poetry is an oral art form and thus it deserves, even demands, to be read aloud. Many poets have grounded themselves more fully in their art form through reciting to an audience. And when listening to poets recite, the audience is often transported by the music of the words and the beauty of the images, or challenged by the experimental approach to form, sound or ideas. These days there are multiple opportunities for poets to recite and listen to others read, from regular series like the long-running Art Bar Poetry Series in Toronto to special events and random guerrilla-style recitations on the street. Many poets begin their reading experience with a stint at an open mic night. Bonnie Nish, who will later speak about running her own series, talks here about what happened when she first got the courage to read her work in public: "The first time I read at an open mic I was so nervous and I read so fast, everyone actually asked me to read my work again. My knees were shaking and as I reread my work it felt as if I had been centre stage for an eternity. This particular crowd was warm and receptive, however, and made me realize how important it is to create a safe atmosphere, especially for newcomers. This feeling is something I have carried with me to create the kinds of events that I produce today."

Catherine Graham from Toronto shares a story about how she used to giggle when doing presentations until the life-altering day she undertook to read poetry aloud:

I was completing an M.A. in creative writing in poetry in Northern Ireland. Together with my fellow M.A. students, I was scheduled to read at a fringe event as part of the Belfast Festival at Queen's. It was fall and I'd spent the summer listening to visiting poets lecture, workshop and read from their books; poets such as Billy Collins, Paula Meehan, Jean Valentine, Medbh McGuckian and Carol Ann Duffy. With such powerful writers as models I wanted to do my best as a reader and I especially didn't want to giggle. I practiced aloud in my small rented cottage by the Irish Sea. I organized the order of poems, knowing exactly what I'd say in between. I imagined the audience sitting in front of me,

not in judgment like I thought my fellow high-school class-
mates were doing, but engaged with the work – letting the
poems' images and rhythms into their hearts and minds. I
was the final reader that night. The bookstore was shadowy
dark from the table-lit candles, giving the audience a tender
moonlight glow. This helped ease my nerves, but the manic
butterflies still slammed against my stomach wall looking
for a way out. When my name was called I took my place
behind the podium and began. The practice had served
me well; the poems so ingrained I barely needed printed
words before me. As the poems unspooled line by line, I
thought deeply about what I was reading. Somehow, the
shy awkward student had stepped aside to let content take
centre stage. I connected with the audience. And most im-
portantly, I didn't giggle.

Reciting poetry for me was, eventually, also a life-changing
practice. When I started writing, I never thought about perform-
ing. A classic introvert (believe it or not), I had never felt the desire
to get up in front of an audience, preferring to compose and recite
to myself in solitude. However, when I was in my later teens, I
started to attend meetings at the Burnaby Writers' Society. Here,
I learned that performing was *de rigueur* if you were a poet of any
ilk! And, my competitive nature stirring after listening to too many
umming and ahhing reciters, I got up at one of the regular events
at the art gallery and read three poems. It was harder than I imag-
ined. Quite an out-of-body experience, as I stuttered through them
rapidly, hands trembling and then sat down fast. Perhaps I wasn't
quite as bad as I thought, though, as invitations to read again kept

coming: from Evelyn Lau, both of us still adolescents at the time, at a happening called "This Ain't No Greasy Kids' Stuff: Poets Under 25"; with Alexandra Oliver and in Victoria, with Patricia Young and P.K. Page, the latter of whom was tremendously gracious to me although I was likely far from mind-blowing as either a poet or performer at that age.

When poets recite they are engaging in a relatively long tradition, but one that became more popular in the mid-twentieth century. Since around 1950, with the advent of Modernism, the frequency of poetry readings has increased. Earlier on in the century, poets like Vachel Lindsay or E. Pauline Johnson would travel on a performance circuit, somewhat in the manner of today's spoken word artists, presenting their recitations, usually accompanied by music, to large crowds in each town. However, they were not the norm. Since the 1960s especially, it has become much more of a requirement for poets to be interested in and proficient at reciting their work. Publishers now expect that a poet, once their book is published, will at the very least undertake a book launch and several local readings. Although funding is minimal, and the geographical range of Canada is often daunting, the publishers are even more thrilled if the poet is able to go on a cross-country tour. Tours are vital to a poet, despite their costs in time, money and energy. On a tour, a poet can not only recite to many audiences who would otherwise be unable to hear them, but can sell books and see other parts of the country.

While many tours are undertaken by plane, bus or car, stopping in major cities and having one or two readings, some poets have gone out of their way to do something a little different, like Vancouverite Kevin Spenst, who set up one hundred randomized, unfunded readings from his chapbooks from Victoria to Toronto. He selected the venues but didn't necessarily promote official readings beforehand. Instead, he just travelled to the location and performed at the allotted hour, sometimes to one audience member, occasionally for many, making money to get to the next venue partially through sales of his chapbooks. Another writer, rob mcclennan from Ottawa, took part in a VIA Rail Canada tour in 1999 and says: "I toured with Anne Stone and Kath MacLean for about five weeks by train. We started in Montreal, and ended up in Victoria. It took a year to plan. We had about a half dozen Canada Council–funded readings. We also got VIA Rail passes and stayed with people for much of the journey." Wendy Morton, of Victoria, went one step further and obtained corporate funding from WestJet and Chrysler, making her seeming audacity appear a simple process with this explanation of how she did it:

One day I got the idea to write poems for people on West-Jet Airlines in exchange for flights. So I called them up and eventually they said yes.

Then I called up Chrysler and asked for a car when I travelled for poetry. They said yes right away.

Then I called up Fuji, asked for a camera, they sent me two.

Then I called up the Royal York, asked for a free room when I was in Toronto. They said yes.

Prairie Naturals Vitamins was my sponsor for years, also AbeBooks.

Poetry has been a great currency for me. I just ask for what I want, and usually I get it.

Then I write the person who says yes a poem.

I say to that, *wow*.

For an even more unusual approach, there's Toronto writer Leigh Kotsilidis, who, along with Linda Besner, Asa Boxer, David Seymour and other poets, toured using a most unusual means of transportation: the canoe. They also steered clear of large cities, tying up their crafts in small towns. Besner explains: "The main stress was to get into parts of the country that none of us know. Most publicity tours hit only major cities. A lot of the canoe poets are from small or mid-sized towns so they understand that residents must often travel distances to see new artists."

Touring leads to contact with a network of poets and, most importantly, multiple recitations from a book honours the aural strengths of the poems within. I have gone on eight cross-Canada tours, one of which, in 2009, involved over twenty-seven events stretching from Victoria, BC, to St. John's, NL, and whether I am having singalongs of the "Ballad of the Metal Men" from my 2012 poetry collection, *Trobairitz*, with small-town seniors or reciting elegies in a Wolfe Island, ON, cemetery as chickens cluck and a donkey brays, I know I am doing something vital to enlarge the art of writing in the world. And in turn, performing has changed me into someone less afraid, more confident in my breath, posture and ability to project in all senses of that word.

# Memorization

*An artist is not just a dreamer.*
– Pitika Ntuli, "Ntuli comes to Museum Africa"


Even less than fifty years ago in North America and Europe, the practice of memorizing poetry and other texts was a common part of the educational system. Today, however, if one is not an actor, it is possible to obtain multiple degrees without having once memorized a poem, never mind having performed a piece as part of literary appreciation or elocution classes. While rote memorization might have been used as a poor shortcut to comprehension, serving more as a source of torture than anything else to those whose strengths weren't language based, the removal of memorization from the educational system wasn't really the wisest idea. It serves to embed poems in one's psyche at an early age, contributing at the same time to what scientists refer to as neural plasticity (Best Colleges Online). In a *New Yorker* article, writer Brad Leithauser summarizes what he feels to be the continued importance of poetic memorization:

> Memorized poems are a sort of larder, laid up against the hungers of an extended period of solitude. . . .
>
> The best argument for verse memorization may be that it provides us with knowledge of a qualitatively and physiologically different variety: you take the poem inside you, into your brain chemistry if not your blood, and you know it at a deeper, bodily level than if you simply read it off a screen. [Catherine] Robson puts the point succinctly: "If we do not learn by heart, the heart does not feel the rhythms of poetry as echoes or variations of its own insistent beat."

I began to memorize poems fairly early. I think Alfred, Lord Tennyson's "The Eagle" was the first one when I was about five, going on to W. B. Yeats' "When You Are Old" and William Carlos Williams' "This is Just to Say." Children memorize much more easily than adults, of course. When, in grade ten, I decided to memorize the whole of Mark Antony's soliloquy from *Julius Caesar* that begins "Friends, Romans, countrymen, lend me your ears," it unrolled smoothly from my tongue; whereas now, while I still memorize sonnets from Robinson Jeffers and Edna St. Vincent Millay among others, trying to memorize Edgar Allan Poe's "The Raven" nearly obliterated my brain cells. Regardless, I continue to make the effort and feel jubilant when I succeed, able then to take the poem with me to the dentist during fillings or on long shifts on a film set. Poems that live in one's blood achieve a true home in the poet.

Many biographies of poets also mention the importance of memorization. In *Sara Teasdale: Woman & Poet*, William Drake quotes an interview where the early twentieth century American writer tells how she used to memorize poems such as Christina Rossetti's "A Christmas Carol" as a child and then "stand by the window during a snowstorm literally enchanted by their music." The beat poet Diane di Prima recounts in her autobiography, *Recollections of My Life as a Woman: The New York Years,* how she was deeply influenced in childhood by a cousin, Liz, who recited poetry to her, particularly "If" by Rudyard Kipling and how di Prima "soon got it by heart" too. Donald Hall also speaks in his memoir, *Unpacking the Boxes: A Memoir of a Life in Poetry,* of how he became enamoured by the poetry of W. H. Auden, showing the depth of his fascination by not only reading all his work but by memorizing pieces, especially, "As I Walked Out One Evening." Robert Frost felt that it was "the utmost of ambition" to memorize poems, to lodge them "where they will be hard to get rid of," while Canadian poet Alice Major discusses the scientific benefits of memorizing poems in her collection *Intersecting Sets: A Poet Looks at Science.* She claims that such acts of memory allow "the brain's neurons [to] lay down small calcium spines that enable a synaptic connection to be made.... An indelibly remembered poem is a flower growing from thorns." Memorizing poetry has historically also been a way to woo women, with Canadian poets like Milton Acorn proving enticing to the poet Gwendolyn MacEwen for, among other talents, his ability to "quote from memory what seemed to be the collected poems of Shelley and Yeats," according to MacEwen's biographer, Rosemary Sullivan.

However, as BC poet Susan McCaslin shares, poets can begin their memorization practice at any time: early on, when time opens up after children leave home or following retirement from a job. Here, she tells us in detail her thoughts on memorization:

> Since retiring from teaching English at a community college in 2007, I've developed a fairly regular practice of memorizing poems while walking in the countryside around Fort Langley. Retiring from my day job has given me the privilege of being a full-time writer and broadening the practices that enhance my writing. Though I feel as busy as ever, as most so-called retired (re-fired) people do, I really do have more time to walk, meditate and attend to the interior workings of poems.
>
> Right now, I'm living with a very active Miniature Australian Shepherd who needs a lot of exercise and pushes me out the door daily. Being in the countryside along the Fraser River provides me with lots of beautiful places to walk. The rhythm of walking and the rhythms of poetry go hand in hand. I can't seem to memorize while sitting at my desk or making supper. Being alone, except for the companionship of my canine friend, is a precondition for effective memorization.

Such a memorization practice was once typical for middle- to upper-class social circles, she remembers:

> My paternal grandmother was a severe but impassioned schoolteacher who believed in learning poems "by rote," as was common in her day. I cried when I heard her whispering lines from [Henry Wadsworth] Longfellow's "A Psalm of Life" on her deathbed: "Dust thou art, to dust returnest,

/ Was not spoken of the soul." Her legacy to me was a well-worn anthology of poems that still falls open at her favourite places.

So I learned from her that memorizing poetry can be heart-work. You impress the poem so intensely into your psyche that it becomes a permanent part of you – mind, emotions, body and all. It can see you through life's big shifts and transitions.

In an age when we are inundated with masses of information, taking time to memorize words we love can become a kind of spiritual practice. It takes work and patience to allow words to penetrate and transform the heart.

I began my practice by working with rhymed and metered poems, "chestnuts" from my childhood and from graduate school that have remained with me. Rhyme is a mnemonic device, so a rhymed poem is generally much easier to commit to memory, at least for me. I plan to move on to free verse next.

While beginning the practice of memorization later in life, as McCaslin suggests, can challenge the "aging brain," leading memorization to take longer and also be interrupted by adult issues like "turmoil, deadlines," she enthuses about its relevance to the practice of writing her own poetry:

What has intensified for me in the process of memorization is the palpable sense of bonding with the heart and mind of the author. At the risk of sounding mystical, I'd say there's a sense of channeling that goes on, whether you interpret that as a literal or metaphorical occurrence. The poet's words instantly take you into the state of mind of the poet at the time of the composing – right inside the poetic process. Why just this word here? Yes, that's right! And that bit of enjambment!

A poet's words are like little perfumeries that release their essence as you re-enact the process of their making. Being with the poem in this way can be a form of communion. In memorizing, there's a sense of co-creating, a joining of your voice to the poet's and to the voices of all those who have read the poem aloud or silently since its conception.

I'm a classic introvert, but memorizing a poem is more like declaiming or acting than quiet reading. While memorizing [Samuel Taylor] Coleridge's "Kubla Khan," I would notice my voice suddenly booming out in unexpected places as if Coleridge himself were prompting, "Give it a big blast here. There, a hush, a whisper." This was not how I had planned to recite.

Then there's the fun of discovering how many ways there are to read a line as the voice plays over the thrumming metrical base. Memorizing allows me to feel in my pulse the rhythms and cadences of the poem. Because it isn't my own poem, I feel freer, less inhibited, more capable of assuming an identity other than that of my phenomenal self.

There's also an excitement when you get to the place where you know the poem so well you don't have to worry about stumbling or forgetting a line or word. Soon the dance begins, the soaring, the play. By painstakingly living with the poem over days or weeks or months, the poem will give itself to you in new ways. You and the poem become intimate.

Often, memorizing a poem awakens new insights into works we thought we knew. When "committing to heart" Emily's Dickinson's "I'm Nobody! Who Are You?," I began to see it not as a statement of self-effacement, but as a Zen koan about the freedom of discovering each of us is a "no self." "How dreary – to be – Somebody," indeed! I'll have breakfast with Emily, this ecstatic rower in paradise, any time and enter the no-self zone.

The final way in which memorizing poems has changed my practice is that it has given me greater confidence, not just in myself, but in my poems, and in poetry itself. For instance, I was at a poetry reading where, for the third time in my life, I stood up to recite a poem. This one was the "Kubla Khan" I had worked so hard to memorize. The crowd was with me and I delivered the poem as if I had stepped inside Coleridge's dream. I felt fearless, fierce, enamoured of the "damsel with a dulcimer," and took the audience with me. I became a woman with "flashing eyes... [and] floating hair" who had "drunk the milk of Paradise." The next day, a friend of mine said, "You know, Susan, I wish you would read your own poems with the same passionate intensity with which you read Coleridge." I realized that my belief in the utter timelessness of Coleridge's art had given me permission to step out, to be transported and to transport. I realized that often when reading my own poems, I'm second-guessing myself. What will they think of this line? Should I be wearing red shoes? Oh, no, I want to change that line. Is that person in the back disengaged or just asleep? And the good news is that since memorizing, I have come to cast off self-doubt and stand behind my words in the honouring of the craft.

Vancouver spoken word artist Chris Gilpin concurs with Susan's newfound confidence in reciting her own poems as a benefit of memorization. Beginning by memorizing other poets when young, he then decided to commit all his own poetry to memory. He states that "to create the correct dramatic impact, memorization becomes necessary. Just as an actor couldn't create the same impact if they came onstage with a script, so too a performance poet will not be able to give the words their due without their full powers of dramatization. It's also a key to connecting with the audience. As Jack McCarthy told me, 'You gotta look the audience in the eye. It keeps them honest.' That's a big part of why I memorize my work."

I also find that memorizing a poem or a song and performing these at the start of readings attracts the audience instantly, channelling them into an "energy zone" that gives the rest of the reading an increased potency.

Catherine Graham agrees that memorizing poetry has significant advantages at readings: "It's very rewarding being the mouthpiece for your work without the barrier of a book between you and the audience. It deepens the intimacy of the experience." She began memorizing with her first book by carrying each poem with her, "during [her] walks around Toronto, repeating the growing sequence over and over, line by line. Not only has this memory work been useful for poetry reading," she claims, "but it has also provided [her] with a focus during challenging situations like being trapped in a metal chamber for an MRI and enduring weeks of radiation treatment. Reciting poems silently helps calm [her] mind." In her work as a teacher she asks students to "memorize a poem of their choosing. Because of the anxiety this challenge often triggers, [she] give[s] them options: one line, one stanza or one short poem. When the day comes to share their memory work, students decide if they'd like their classmates to listen with eyes open or closed. That way they won't feel so self-conscious when reciting."

Glen Sorestad, a Saskatoon poet, connects memorization, especially of poetry, to the development of the poet. He suggests:

[It is] like planting seeds into the consciousness of anyone who is at all creative . . . I am not alone among poets in being able to recall lines of poetry from the past, usually with considerable pleasure, and I know beyond a shadow of a doubt that this store of internalized poetry is something that probably informs my sensibilities and my semi-consciousness, so that when I am writing I have no idea how my choice of words or the rhythmic shape the line is taking may, in fact, be informed by what lies there in that unconscious cache of sounds and words and phrases and images and lines. But I know it is there and I know that it is, in some mysterious and perhaps osmosis-like fashion, influencing what I write.

I think, too, that the poet who has spent time memorizing many lines of poetry is necessarily, through this process of memorizing and (presumably) reciting those lines, become more attuned to the sound of the ebb and flow of poetic lines, probably without ever having had the benefit of a prosody class or having studied [Paul] Fussell's *Poetic Meter and Poetic Form*. If we as poets generally accept the premise that a poet's apprenticeship should begin long before he / she tries to write poetry and that reading a vast amount and diversity of poems is a starter, or at the very least should go hand in hand with the first attempts to write poetry, then I would say that a certain amount of memorization and recitation could well be one of the important building blocks in the apprenticeship of a poet.

Amanda Jernigan adds that "memorization is a natural outgrowth of a life in poetry, whether that life is as a reader only or as reader and writer both: the great poems announce themselves as great precisely because they stay with you, in whole or in part; they allow you to carry them with you through your life."

She feels that learning to recite poems goes far beyond just acquiring a skill as "it is a delight both to receive a poem from the memory of another and to be able to offer a poem from one's own memory, in return: it allows one to be part of an ancient commerce, like the sharing of food. And memorized poems can be a comfort in extremis: we know that death will take everything from us, in the end, but it seems that memorized poems – especially those memorized in childhood – can be among the last things left to us."

Yet while some people seem to simply have the knack of being able to memorize easily, most of us struggle with it. Even writers who agree that memorization is important, like the American poet Mark Strand, can admit that the practice has been challenging for them, unlike his parents who, Strand claims, "remembered the poems they'd learned as children. . . . [My father would] memorize what he read. . . . [He] used to say [it was] a way of reaching places that he couldn't scratch . . . [and how] he entered into rapture" ("The Uncontrollable Elements"). Often our belief that we can't memorize due to the lack of experience we have exercising this ability can prevent us from even attempting to learn a few pieces of poetry by heart. Yet, as another American poet, Christie Ann Reynolds, emphasizes, "I think if we want to be responsible writers, we should commit to knowing a few pieces that live inside of us, not only in a book."

But memorizing poetry doesn't have to be an overwhelming task. In an article for the *New York Times* in 2009, writer Jim Holt explained his method for learning poetry by heart:

> The key to memorizing a poem painlessly is to do it incrementally, in tiny bits. I knock a couple of new lines into my head each morning before breakfast, hooking them onto what I've already got. At the moment, I'm 22 lines into Tennyson's "Ulysses," with 48 lines to go. It will take me about a month to learn the whole thing at this leisurely pace, but in the end I'll be the possessor of a nice big piece of poetical real estate, one that I will always be able to revisit and roam about in.
>
> The process of memorizing a poem is fairly mechanical at first. You cling to the meter and rhyme scheme (if there is one), declaiming the lines in a sort of sing-songy way without worrying too much about what they mean.

It helps to remember that memorizing poems is no different than memorizing songs. All of us have countless song lyrics in our minds and yet few of us can claim to have memorized a poem. The reason is at least twofold: songs are all around us in our popular media and poems sadly aren't; and there is an expectation of song memorization that is not given to poems in our society. Songs, after all, usually still rhyme and, also, lyrics are a much more social form than poems; several people in your circle might have the same song memorized, but it's highly unlikely more than one will have memorized the same poem. Thus, while I have certainly felt at least lines from poems get "stuck in my head" like James Merrill's "Again last night I dreamed the dream called Laundry" ("The Mad Scene"), or Kenneth Patchen's "lilies, locking and singing / in the bone" ("Eight Early Poems"), I rarely share this with anyone while a popular song lyric can simply pop out at work, for instance, and usually find a co-memorizer to sing along with.

Amanda Jernigan sums up this discussion by quoting musician Arlo Guthrie:

As for how to learn something by heart? The only method I know is what Arlo Guthrie calls, with justice, the boring method, saying to his concert audience, "Okay, now, repeat after me …" When you're learning from a book, you repeat after the book, of course, not the bard, but the process is much the same: read and repeat, read and repeat, phrase by phrase or line by line as your memory permits. I find it helps to actually say the words out loud, though this isn't strictly necessary; one can say them "aloud to one's self," if circumstances advise against noise.

And of course, she adds, "Pattern is the friend of memory: so rhyme, metre, alliteration – any sort of repetition, even if irregularly used – will be your allies. It's also wise to pay attention not only to the poetic unit of the line but to the syntactic units of the phrase, the clause, the sentence: because sense is also an aid to memorization. Further, when reciting poetry from memory, accuracy is the highest virtue; but next, if you forget a word, is the ability to ad lib!"

As Elizabeth Bishop once wrote in a letter on December 19, 1965, "memorizing poetry helps people to have lines recur once in a while all the rest of their lives (and thus the poem dignifies experiences)."

# Research

*Poetry is a profession which engages the entire being of the artist.*
– Stephen Kessler, *Moving Targets*


The writing of poems can be a very personal act. Poems emerge from the poet's life and the perspective may often be of the poet's self or the lyric *I*. Yet all poets are formed by a range of teachers, human and otherwise. Many are found in the books we read, books whose influence sometimes yields immediate results and other times take years to make their impact felt. We can seek out these texts or they can organically and mysteriously seem to find us. I became obsessed with research-based poems this way. A book called *I, Eternal Child*, filled with Impressionist poems by the painter Egon Schiele, appeared to leap out at me from the library shelves one day and I became completely immersed in seeking out texts on his life and work. This resulted in my first trade book, *Somatic: The Life and Work of Egon Schiele*, in 1998.

Of course, poets over the centuries have researched sources and then braided those stories and facts into their work. Victorian-era poet Alfred, Lord Tennyson used a wide range of subject matter in his poetry, ranging from medieval legends to classical myths, material he likely researched in the course of his studies. Twentieth-century American poet Marianne Moore was also renowned for using research material as the core of her poems. Everything from colour theory to zoology nourished her work. Several of her poems – like her famous piece, "Poetry" – embed quotations from her research; in this case, Leo Tolstoy, W. B. Yeats, William Blake and possibly Kenneth Grahame's *The Wind in the Willows*.

Canadian poetry is full of poems that draw upon research to explore our history. These collections often help us to appreciate the past, to challenge our current perceptions and to rethink our commonly held historical beliefs. Poetry books like Margaret Atwood's *The Journals of Susanna Moodie*, Daphne Marlatt's *Steveston* or Fred Wah's *Diamond Grill* reassess pioneers, landscapes and immigrants in engaging ways that urge us to "re-feel" our relationship with history.

The four Canadian poets I spoke to about research and poetry were passionate about the place that delving into a range of scientific and anthropological source material holds in their work. Theresa Kishkan, a writer who lives in Madeira Park, BC, told me that:

In recent years, I've found myself resisting the usual boundaries of genre. As a gardener, I'm interested in what happens when cross-pollination occurs. I'm also interested in growing everything together – vegetables, flowers, herbs, aromatics, medicinal plants. I want to know about the biology, the ethnobotany, the use and history, and the interconnectedness of plants with human communities. And what I'm pursuing in my work is analogous. I'm trying to find a form that allows me to make room for natural history, human history, travel writing, moments of lyrical expression in the context of exposition (and vice versa), cartography, limnology, deep ecology, exploration of textile history and culture, and so on.

Adam Dickinson sees research as a "kind of complement, in the linguistic and cultural realm, to what scientific research explores in physical and chemical realms." With his latest book, *The Polymers*, along with his next, in which he tests himself for chemicals and microbes, then writes about the results, Dickinson is compelled by how his poetry can enlarge the field of ecopoetics by "shifting traditional, perhaps calcified frames of signification," emphasizing how he wants "poetry to make these giant and seemingly incongruous leaps, especially if we are to imagine solutions to some of the pressing environmental problems of our time – we have to look in unlikely places and at unusual patterns of information." Dickinson's current mode of researching involves "comprehensive study" of his own body, which he is analyzing for trace levels of chemicals, along with addressing its "cultural and linguistic" sites and thereby re-entering the poem as a place to articulate these "apparently disparate systems of knowledge," science and poetry.

Saskatchewan poet, Mari-Lou Rowley would relate to Dickinson's approach, given that she is also a science-based writer. She begins by taking an overview of why she first started writing and then delves into how her rational capacities for thought, analysis and synthesis, along with her scientific and mathematical abilities, feed her art:

I have been writing science-inspired poetry for over two decades, but recently, I realized that my interest in science really came out of an aptitude for mathematics. Ever since I was a child I have been fascinated with shapes, patterns and numbers. In high school I was on contract for all of my math courses; I did the work on my own and checked into class once a week. In the resulting spare time I explored the library.

Nearly four decades later, I began reading Stephen Hawking's *God Created the Integers*. His book, and many of the science articles I have written, triggered a new manuscript of poetry, "NumenRology." These poems not only explore my interest in mathematics, but also some of the obstacles that prevented me from pursuing a career in science, and why the poet emerged instead.

For Rowley, "Poetry is a way of seeing, comprehending and being in, and of, the world. Poetic emergence – the process of bringing a poem into being – requires 'code duality' at several levels: physiological and intellectual, intuition and honed craft, the sensual and the cerebral, awe and wonder anchored by rigour and investigation. My research, fragments of technical language and intertextual play are all techniques to nudge the poem into being."

Patricia Young, a poet from Victoria, BC, describes how poetry itself, rather than scholarship, called her to the process of research, specifically, in her case, on the life cycles and mating habits of animals and birds. Research, she states, altered both the content and tenor of her poetry, enabling her to continue her fascination with language while the work shifted from her own life to the world around her.

In the past I wrote poetry primarily out of personal experience and therefore did not need to do, or was not much interested in doing, research. I might have looked up the qualities of a gum tree, for example, or how waves are formed or cement is made. And I might have woven these bits of information into a poem, but they were rarely the heart of it.

In the past few years, however, I have been working on poems that take as their starting point the mating habits of various fish, insects, birds and mammals. Some research has been necessary to write these (I have to admit) anthropomorphic poems. I call it "research," but it feels more like a treasure hunt. My process is simple: I begin by reading about and around a particular mammal (or insect or fish or bird) until some aspect of its creaturely-ness catches my interest or triggers a response. When I say "read about and around" I don't mean I read in-depth Ph.D. theses. I am just looking for compelling but bare-bones facts. Once I have enough of these facts, I play around with them and see where the poem takes me.

An example: not long ago I began reading up on the sloth, an animal I knew very little about – its biological makeup, metabolism, diet, environment, mating habits, how they raise their young and so on, and in the process came across a single reference to a "slothmidden." What a terrific word, I thought. Though the sloth's sight and hearing are weak, its sense of smell is, apparently, strong, so a slothmidden is a place where male and female sloths find each other to mate. The word *slothmidden*, then, was the gateway into a poem, the first line of which is "I am going to the midden to meet my lover."

After writing about the slowest animal I could think of, I decided to try to write one about the fastest animal – or bird – I could think of – the hummingbird. Again, searching for an entrance (or a bit of treasure), I came across the lovely word – *lek* – which is the term for the song male birds sing to woo a female. This, in itself, was an amazing fact – that up to forty males will sing to a single female.

Young notes how, in relation to research, the Internet has been more a boon than a bane:

The Internet can be a terrible distraction. It can be argued that it has been bad for writers, primarily in terms of siphoning off deep concentration. But the Internet has also provided writers access to a vast store of information easily and quickly. I might have written these poems without the Internet – a set of good encyclopedias would have been almost as useful – but I certainly wouldn't have been able to observe live animals in the kind of detail afforded me watching them on YouTube. David Attenborough's footage, as well as his commentary, of an Australian bowerbird is a wonderful example.

I like this animal/mating project because I don't know what I will find when I start prowling around sites such as Live Science or *National Geographic*. I don't know how a poem will take shape, if it will speak in the voice of an animal and, if so, what the attitude of that animal will be.

What I do know is that I am pleasantly surprised (and relieved) that my own life is no longer the focus of my poetry.

Undoubtedly, I agree with Patricia. After my first book on Schiele many of my collections emerged from research, whether into extinct species; Mattie Gunterman, the pioneer photographer; trobairitzes (for which I travelled to France and Turkey) or even cross-cultural representations of grief for my most recent book, 2014's *Designated Mourner*. Research broadened my work beyond personal perspectives and allowed me to dive into material that I found fascinating. When you decide to undertake a course of research through books, the Internet or other sources, your reading practices become more focused, deepen, may even become obsessive like mine did. Recreating those facts through the imaginative channel of poems is how I communicate my obsessions to audiences and readers. Thoroughly drenching oneself in the subject matter, whether it's Aztec culture or the life of the sculptor Auguste Rodin, ensures that you are more likely to comprehend the material with complexity and feeling and be able to transform it into art through the power of language.

# Writing Reviews and Criticism

*The demands upon you, as a writer, are far greater than you could have guessed when you filled out your application form and mailed it. How far are you willing to travel this love you profess to have for words?*
– Mary Ruefle, *Madness, Rack, and Honey*

Not only did books of poems stick in my mind early on, but the reviews I read of them and the reputations of particular reviewers also made (and continue to make) their impact felt. It could be Helen Vendler critiquing Robinson Jeffers in ad hominem fashion (dubbing him "a friendless, freakish boy... preoccupied with recording" in *The New Yorker*, in 1988, long after Jeffers' death). Or, closer to home, it could be the scholarly thoroughness of Northrop Frye represented by his yearly poetry surveys from "Letters in Canada," published in *The Toronto Quarterly* from 1951 to 1960. Contemporary, often caustic, poetry critics like Carmine Starnino, Zachariah Wells and the inimitable Judith Fitzgerald are compelling too. (In the latter's 2010 review of Evelyn Lau's *Living Under Plastic*, for instance, she claims it "rarely rises to the poetic occasion...[and] all too often collapses beneath the weight of its precious pondering of imponderabilities.")

In the literary magazines that still publish reviews, like *The Fiddlehead*, *The Malahat Review* and *ARC Poetry Magazine*, it is the review section I turn to after reading the poetry, interested to see what books have been selected and how their critics will balance praises with demands. Often these reviews will lead me to purchase a book or review it myself. I have written reviews for about twelve years, first for college newspapers and magazines like *The Journal of Canadian Poetry*, then for *Canadian Notes & Queries* and *Canadian Literature* and more recently on my own blog, now called *Marrow Reviews*. When reviews emerge on my own books (even when they are humorously absurd like the one Lynn Crosbie wrote for *The National Post* in 1999 on *Somatic* in which she suggested my poems were "Rorschach blots" and that I should receive an award called "I can make anything seem perverted!"), I am compelled by the critic's engagement with the work, fascinated to see what mattered to them, and how and where I fell short in my ability to communicate with my craft.

The value poetry possesses as an art form and to society is shaped, at least partially, by whether it is given space in publications, and time and energy from publishers and critics. While more online and even print magazines have been springing up that publish poems, few in comparison print reviews or critical essays on new or reconsidered collections, never mind the genre of poetry itself.

"Book reviews in Canada are becoming an increasingly rare art form," laments Bronwyn Kienapple in *Torontoist* before introducing a new venue for criticism, *The Toronto Review of Books*. While books are still reviewed, more often than not, the reviews appear online, on websites for journals and magazines that used to be print based or, more commonly, on personal blogs and sites like Goodreads or Amazon. These latter assessments are usually written by readers who rarely provide in-depth critique of a text, merely stating whether they liked it or didn't. Newspapers have all made severe cuts to their book review sections and supposedly review-based publications, like *BC BookWorld*, no longer offer a regular section that critiques poetry books, but rather offer mere overviews. In the past Susan Musgrave and Hannah Main-van der Kamp served as hosts introducing readers to six or so new titles every issue. We've lost the tradition of writers frequently reviewing their contemporaries' single books or entire oeuvres, sad even when the reviews were frequently dismissive or downright rude (witness Truman Capote on Jack Kerouac: "That's not writing, that's typing").

Part of the problem is the abundance of poetry books being produced by presses in general. Having so many new collections can overwhelm the possibility of criticism. Northrop Frye prided himself on reviewing *every* single book of poetry produced that year, a number of texts that would be impossible for twenty such critics to review reasonably now. The masses of books released every season can lead to reactions of indifference, lassitude or cynicism about the likelihood of any of them mattering in the long run or even in the short term. Critics are also much less sure now which books to review and where to place them if they do. Further, while reviewing used to make a partial living for a renowned critic like

Anthony Burgess who, "by the mid-80s … was getting £600 for each 1,000-word piece … and writing up to 40 reviews a year" (Morrison), it has now become a hobby, hard to fit in amidst all the other demands on one's time. The irony is, of course, that a strong group of reviewers could weed out this surplus and help define more clearly what constitutes the significant poetry of the era. "The purpose of poetry reviewing is to keep the art of poetry alive," says Kevin Prufer, a poet, editor and prolific reviewer for a variety of literary magazines in the States. "It's vital for our culture that we not only publish good poetry, but that we continue to sort out for ourselves what exactly *good* poetry is" (quoted in Teicher).

Daniel Zomparelli addresses an offshoot of this issue in his preface to the first issue of his magazine, *Poetry is Dead*: "One of the other reasons poetry is getting squished out is the oversaturation of the industry: there are too many poets and not enough readers. There are countless poets – online poets, part-time poets and spoken word poets – who are all trying to obtain a bit of fame, but not purchasing poetry books, journals or magazines. Ask any poetry editor about the volume of submissions they receive, and they will tell you that they can't keep up with them. Ask about sales, on the other hand, and they will tell you that they are miniscule."

Another part of the problem is that many contemporary poets tend to either fear the potential repercussions of writing criticism or dismiss the importance of reviews with some variant of the "it will all come out in the wash" statement. They feel that time will make wise judgments as to the value of what is created in any culture, an improbable feat if a critical vocabulary isn't developed, through which poetry is reviewed according to such elements as syntax, rhythm and form. As Thomas M. Disch notes, poets embedded in academe often worry about offending their peers and threatening their chances for tenure, and consider critical reviews "bad form." Due to the poetry scene being small and highly interconnected in Canada, poets can be resistant to writing reviews because they worry about offending their peers, who may be on juries capable of either giving or withholding grants, teaching positions or awards. The result is that countless books of poetry emerge every year that don't even receive one review, and when a review is written it is more likely to be an overview instead. Whole poetic vocations can pass without a single critical essay being composed on the poet's overall vision.

In the past, there were fewer books produced, enabling poets to more readily assess literary output. Frye, in 1958, as stated, was able to review all the trade books of poetry published in Canada in that quarter of the year: fifteen. Today, the numbers are much higher as Scott Griffin points out each spring when he announces how many books he has received for the Griffin Award (376! 491!), a number that would seem to make reviewing, and judging, near impossible. Conversely, when e. e. cummings' *Collected Poems* came out in 1938, he not only received reviews from Ezra Pound, Carl Sandburg and Marianne Moore among other fellow poets, but he was the subject of a survey essay by another poet, John Peale Bishop. These reviews were not always positive; in fact, he was the recipient of much castigation, as with this quote from poet and critic Yvor Winters who spluttered, "In the work of Cummings, the artistry which gives dignity . . . is entirely lacking" (quoted in Sawyer-Lauçanno). Regardless of tenor, reviews and criticism brought cummings' work to public attention and secured the poet's place as one worthy of consideration within poetic history. Of course, in that era, the small number of books published meant that diversity in gender and race was often lacking. To represent the variety of work produced today we would need every student in all the M.F.A. programs in this country to dedicate themselves to composing reviews, as well as for magazines to again pay for reviews rather than expecting them to always be written for nothing more than a complimentary copy of the journal, too tiny an incentive for many.

People who now write reviews do so for a different range of reasons: to bring other poets' work to greater prominence and contribute to shaping the literary canon or, less altruistically, to draw attention to one's own name, stir up the poetic pot a little and otherwise generate discussion and its concomitant energy.

Five Canadian poets who write reviews and criticism on a regular basis – Susan Glickman, Jay Ruzesky, M. Travis Lane, Bruce Meyer and Dennis E. Bolen – spoke to me about why they take the risk of being opinionated in relation to poetry. Susan Glickman, who lives in Toronto, recounts how she loves "taking stuff apart to see how it works; as a critic, I look at artistic influences, and aesthetic theories, and historical contexts, and so on, all of which bring larger dimensions to whatever I'm reading. That is, as a critic, I never see a work as simply *sui generis* but as a product of its time and place as well as that particular author." She also adds that "being a critic has helped me hone a vocabulary and methodology for reviewing my own work."

Vancouver Island poet Jay Ruzesky agrees, emphasizing that when he writes reviews, he benefits by getting "a better sense of the range and scope of the writing that is happening in Canada and that helps me feel connected." Further, he remarks that, as "Thelonious Monk said, 'You rehearse every time you play on the instrument,' so writing anything . . . is still part of the practice of writing." He adds, "When I'm writing reviews, I'm usually given a deadline . . . [and] I think deadlines . . . could be good for writers."

M. Travis Lane, a poet from New Brunswick who has been writing reviews for over fifty years, has many firm opinions on the art form. Calling the composition, and, at times, the reception of reviews "a private and lonely occupation," Lane believes that the poet does indeed take risks in reviewing their contemporaries. She suggests that review writing is often "a good way of engaging with poetry," but that it can sometimes put one at odds with the writing community at large. She expands: "To engage with the poetry community is to go to places, to read aloud, to meet people, to workshop, to teach and network. I write reviews for the sake of poetry – for the sake of the poetry I recommend – not for the community per se." Having written reviews since she was a graduate student, Lane feels strongly that "the reviewer should not only have the choice of which books she wants to read carefully, she also should have the choice of deciding which books can be meaningfully and intelligently compared to each other." And further, a review should have some breadth and depth, featuring "room for quotations so the reviewer can demonstrate what she means – this helps the reader decide whether he might agree with the reviewer or not." While, personally speaking, she doesn't think that reviews have affected her poetic development in any serious sense, she nonetheless underlines the importance of reading careful, considerate reviews of one's work because "a review means to a poet 'Gosh! Somebody has actually read the damn book!'" Further, she admits that writing reviews "makes one aware of how much good poetry is being written."

Bruce Meyer from Barrie suggests that "reviewing should be a way to offer constructive feedback about what one has learned about the art from another poet." He recalls that he began "reviewing poetry simply out of a need to learn more – and to illumine another poet's work. There is a kind of moon-like reflective process that comes from book reviewing, especially when the reviewer gets his ego out of the way." Good reviewing practices, he claims, include, "objectivity, testing personal ideas against the ideas on the page, and asking those key questions about how and what and why a poet has done something well or poorly." Writing reviews, Meyer notes, "taught me a lot about poetry and helped me add more tools to my own workbench." He gives reviewing assignments to writing workshop students so they can understand more about their own work by trying to learn more about someone else's, emphasizing that "poetry is a continual learning process and reviewing is one of the classrooms a poet must visit."

Another writer who has just released his first book of poetry (though he has published many novels) and recently taken up the art of reviewing, Dennis E. Bolen, from Vancouver, has this to contribute about his nascent experience as a poetic critic. He says he began reviewing

to assist the book trade generally and specifically help fellow writers. Also, there can be somewhat of a financial incentive. More importantly, in terms of community, I think the greater the sharing of opinion and assistance we spread among each other the better. I would say that since I took up verse, three years or so ago, I've enjoyed the writing life much more than I ever did as a fiction figure. Come to think of it, despite a ten-fold greater financial income as a fiction writer, I was miserable. My theory is that poets know there is no money, so they get by on the joy of expression and the companionship of austerity, while fiction writers are all arguing over the five-dollar bill on the table.

When I asked if he would recommend this practice to all poets, he replied, "Reviewing, and all the concomitant challenges attached to the practice, may not be for everyone. But I do encourage any-one with experience and knowledge to consider it as the literary world direly requires the review form to both educate readers (and writers) and publicize work. Art, I always say, does not live inside its simple existence, but in the minds and responses of its audience members."

Composing reviews and criticism is clearly a beneficial prac-tice for both the writers and for their subject matter, as well as for the health of the poetry scene in this geographically vast country. Without the reviews that appear in literary magazines like *ARC* and *Contemporary Verse 2* (*CV2*), zines like *Broken Pencil* and newspaper-style publications like *Pacific Rim Review of Books*, how many poets from BC would know about books released by writers in New-foundland or even Saskatchewan?

As mentioned earlier, one of the reasons writers overall are resistant to writing reviews is because their criticism could be con-strued as negative, a charge that has led many literary journals to only accept reviews that veer toward praise or merely overview the book without taking a stance at all. Poet Jan Zwicky asserts in a *Canadian Women in the Literary Arts* essay that when she "was review editor for *The Fiddlehead* in the early nineties, [she] made a point of requesting that a review be written only if the reviewer was genuinely enthusiastic about the book." Nervousness about how the review will impact on the writer is a real concern (apparently Phyllis Webb stopped writing after a series of biting reviews by uncomprehending male reviewers in the '70s), but I think this fear is crippling our ability to read books with an open mind. I decided a long time ago that if awards and jobs depended on me keeping my mouth shut then I didn't want them. Aiming always for balance in every book I review, I have still been accused by some writers of being negative, of wanting to "tear down" rather than to "boost." Such accusations come with the territory of being a reviewer and, mostly, don't need to be taken seriously if your intent is clear.

Poets have varying opinions on the nature of the "negative" review. Robert Pinsky, in *The Poetry Porch*, suggests that "reviewing may be most appropriate for young poets rather than older ones. It is maybe best performed by someone who is setting out to survey the field in a spirit driven by the future . . . and someone who does not yet know too many people personally. I don't think negative reviews should be written of a first book, or of a little-known author: if unknown work is bad, let it sink of its own weight." Jan Zwicky's perspective is similar, as she stated in her sharply contested essay on the ethics of the negative review: "Grousing about poorly executed work is usually counterproductive," and there is "no need to sharpen the hatchets when a deathly critical silence would do all the public work that needed doing."

Four other poets quoted in Craig Teicher's article on the *Publishers Weekly* website weigh in with different perspectives. Kevin Prufer asserts, "Negative reviews help poetry. We articulate our values about any art as strongly by saying why an example might fail as we do by praising successes." However, there are not many negative reviews published: "I conducted an informal poll of poetry reviews and found that 92% of them were entirely positive, with not one note of criticism."

By contrast, Matthew Zapruder is against negative reviews, stating emphatically, "I'm not interested in the reviewer's opinion about the work, especially if it comes from some unspoken locus of aesthetic authority. The point of view of one critic is particularly important to maintaining aesthetic standards and getting poets to write better. Reviews aren't for writers, but for readers."

Taking another approach is Nickole Brown: "I'm of the school that no publicity is bad publicity. . . . If a book is worth its salt, it's going to attract attention, good and bad. A scathing review might temporarily wound the writer's ego, but if it's bad enough, it might incite readers to pick up the book and judge for themselves." This was the case recently when Barbara Kay harshly critiqued Raziel Reid's YA story of a transgender teen as a "values-void novel" that only "wasted tax dollars," thereby leading sales of the book to sky-rocket overnight.

Timothy Donnelly says that negative reviews need to be smart to work: "negative reviews [can be] ultimately embarrassing and ruinous for everyone, no matter how exciting they might be to read or gossip about. But when a reviewer manages to point out a book's shortcomings evenhandedly, with care and dignity, and with an eye to raising the bar a little higher for readers and for writers, too – that's another story. I'd love to see more reviews like that."

# Translating Other Poets

*It is not my work that interests me above all else; it is work, without a possessive pronoun, that must live, even if our personal contributions are consumed in it.*
– George Seferis, "From a Poet's Journal"


Almost at the same time I discovered poetry in English, I uncovered it in other languages. As I can read French, I bought an anthology of French poets with English translations so I could compare different versions of Arthur Rimbaud, Charles Baudelaire, Guillaume Apollinaire and others, while continuing to add to my vocabulary. In university, I spent time working on translations of French poets on my own as an exercise in comprehending diction and rhythmic choices. Years after, when writing *Trobairitz*, a book that partially concerns the troubadour poets, I translated some poems from *langue d'oc* in order to more fully enter their *fin'amor* idioms. In my twenties I was gifted with Robert Bly's translations of Rainer Maria

Rilke and, later, I found the same poems translated by Edward Snow. It struck me how disparate different translators could be in their intent. The former was concerned with being accessible and modern; the latter on keeping as close as possible to the original German rhyme scheme and form.

When I started reading translations, they seemed relatively transparent to me and I was readily caught up in the sense that I was entering their world. Now, the process of translation appears complex, a difficult art always straining toward the ineffable transformation, more so in dead languages, such as that used by Sappho (although Anne Carson has admirably attempted this feat), than in living and thus more flexible ones like Japanese. Over the past few years I have seen translations of my work in Turkish done by a friend, in Korean by a magazine editor and a whole book, *Caneide (30 sonetti in cagnesco)*, in Italian by the translator Ada Donati. Working with Donati, I realized how many of the words I had carefully selected, particularly the neologisms, were completely untranslatable. We had many discussions about what words to use in their place so as not to entirely alter the meaning. Of course, the unique music of a poem can never be completely translated.

I feel that translation is one of the most challenging acts one can undertake as a writer. As Marc Plourde notes in his essay, "On Translating Miron," in the collection *The Insecurity of Art: Essays on Poetics*, "The translator cannot live in the author's skin, but his work must create the illusion that he does." Translators often know the language they are translating from well, but many translators of poetry are poets who don't necessarily comprehend the language they are working with. Instead they use a translator and a dictionary and then apply their own particular sensitivity for the poetic craft to the labour of translation. If you know the particular language then the process is slightly easier but even then a range of decisions must be made for every poem in terms of the selection of diction, cadence and rhyme scheme. Each poem requires the poet to choose whether the original poem's metre will be as closely followed as possible or if the goal will be to approximate the meaning and thus sacrifice aural qualities of the original piece. Regardless, the translated piece will be, in a sense, an entirely new creation in English than it was in its former language. The poet who wishes to translate, whether from a language they know into English or from a language they need a dictionary and a phrase book to comprehend, must approach the practice with a deep respect for languages and an excessive amount of patience. And the process can even be fun, according to American poet Mark Strand in this interview for *The Paris Review* with playwright Wallace Shawn:

### Shawn

I know that you know your way around quite a few languages – Spanish, Portuguese and Italian, at least – and you've done a certain amount of translating. Has that experience been valuable to you in regard to your own writing?

### Strand

Translating is almost like a game. It is a serious game, because, finally, it's your reading of another poet's work. But you develop a sense of syntactical possibility – you make choices, you have to say to yourself, when you're translating, Should I do it this way, or should I do it that way? When you're writing your own work, you're not asking yourself those questions. Maybe at some much later stage in the writing of a poem, you may say to yourself, objectively, I need a two-syllable word here, with the accent on the first syllable. The line should end here, instead of there. There should be a slant rhyme, some assonance, or something here. . . . But when you're writing, at the beginning, when you're writing, you're not asking yourself those questions. When you're translating, you always are.

Poet Robert Fitzgerald, in an interview with Edward Honig that originally appeared in *The Poet's Other Voice: Conversations on Literary Translation*, reveals his own translation process in terms of how the desire to change a poem from another language to English seems to come from within the poem itself:

One finds in poems and language some quality one appropriates for oneself and wishes to reproduce. So, for years I had in my head certain lines of François Villon, which I first came across in 1931 when I was a student here at Harvard. I found the lines turning into a ballade in English in 1940, after nine years of knocking around in my head, of being heard there in French. Words began to appear in English and to make some kind of equivalent. For what satisfaction it is hard to say, except that something seems unusually piercing, living, handsome, in another language, and since English is yours, you wish it to be there too.

And the American poet Stanley Kunitz once commented positively in a 1977 *Paris Review* interview by Chris Busa that: "Every poet I've ever translated has taught me something. One of the perils of poetry is to be trapped in the skin of your own imagination and to remain there all your life. Translation lets you crack your own skin and enter the skin of another. You identify with somebody else's imagination and rhythm, and that makes it possible for you to become other. It's an opening towards transformation and renewal."

Another American poet, Marilyn Hacker, in an interview with the journal *Barzakh*, is adamant regarding the importance of translating in relation to developing poetic skills:

KCO : In what way does translation, a practice that encourages thoroughness and precision and involves the transcription of another's consciousness, intersect with your poetry?

MH : Translation is always an excellent exercise in creating poetry with one's own ego – and the resonances of one's own experiences or opinions – removed, while one attempts to be as aware as possible of the resonances of the initial text . . . translation gives the poet the opportunity to write poems s/he would otherwise never have written – and syntactic structures, vocabulary, even thought processes found in the close reading necessary for translation are often the jumping-off point of one's own poems.

So even though the Hawaiian poet W. S. Merwin refers to the "utter impossibility of the enterprise" of translation ("Translator's Notes"), it is perhaps the very ineffability of the act that keeps him and others attempting to find equivalent words and similarly resonant sounds. D. G. Jones, in his essay titled "The Grounds for

Translation," sums up the challenge in this way: "It is precisely through translation, that is, inevitably, the mis-translation, the mis-reading, that the poet...manages to find nourishment, manages to avoid being locked in 'the prison house of language.'" Kenneth Koch compares translating and reading translated poetry as a form of trav-elling, an "uncertain and irregular vehicle" but when done well, one full of "marvelous things." As Stephen Kessler sums it up: "This is not a field for the faint of heart, though anyone is free to try their hand [at translating] and learn a lot from the process." Translation is a way of enlarging the possibilities of poetry across time, space and cultures.

In Canada, translations of poetry from French to English have been undertaken quite frequently, the work of D. G. Jones on Paul-Marie Lapointe as one example. (*The 5th Season* from 1985 is one of my favourite poetry translations ever.) Recently, more interest in translating from First Nation languages has been expressed, with poets like Gregory Scofield interweaving his poems in English with translations into Cree. Poets like A. F. Moritz or Erin Mouré have focused on translating the work of Ludwig Zeller or Chus Pato; oth-ers like George McWhirter have released an anthology of Mexican poets called *Where Words Like Monarchs Fly*. Presses like Biblioasis, Quattro Books, Exile Editions and ECW all publish literary transla-tions. House of Anansi Press recently created an imprint, Arachnide Editions, devoted to publishing books from French Canada, though few of these will be poetry. At Wolsak and Wynn, conversely, all the translations they've undertaken have been poetry from contempo-rary poets, in countries such as Argentina, Brazil and Estonia. In 2014, *The Malahat Review* published an issue devoted to translation called "At Home in Translation," featuring a wide array of poets and writers, including Croatian and Romanian. In 2011, the Canada

Council established the Translation Rights Fair in which Québécois and English Canadian presses meet to increase publication opportunities. The number of grant-supported translations is rising. In 2008–09, *The National Post* reports, the council funded sixty-two translations, only twenty-one of which were French to English.

While knowing the language well from which you plan to translate is preferable, it's not essential. I spoke about this aspect of translation with Kingston, ON, poet and novelist Steven Heighton, who reveals a few insights into his own process:

With French poetry, and sometimes with German and Spanish, when I find a poem I like, I take a run at translating it using only a dictionary. After I finish the first draft, I start looking at other people's translations, and sometimes I consult friends who are fluent in the languages (my French is decent, but I really can't speak German or Spanish at all, though I can work my way through an easy poem if I go slowly and have a dictionary at hand). Often, after the third draft or so, I'll begin taking greater liberties, semantically and in terms of structure and diction, since my goal is to create a powerful approximation of the original, which can also stand up as an English poem; so if there's anything in the translation that *feels* translated, I'll do whatever I have to do – reconfiguring an image slightly; finding a better, more kinetic English verb than the one that literally translates the original – to make the poem feel *English*, and alive.

In Heighton's book *Patient Frame*, he includes some of his translations of poets such as Pablo Neruda and Ōnakatomi no Yoshinobu.

Steve Noyes, a poet and fiction writer from Victoria, has gone one step further and steeped himself in two languages, Chinese and Arabic, that he chooses to translate passages or whole poems from into English. He describes some of the difficulties and beauties of each of these languages:

With Chinese, I was intrigued by a different writing system, the characters that are part picture, part symbol and part code, but also by the tones, and the sweet puncturing sounds of this highly compressed language, wherein four characters can say a great deal, can be metonymy for a whole story. Chinese poetry simply evokes the image; doesn't explain it; even the speaker must be inferred. The Chinese language is full of compression, doubling effects and economy.

With Arabic, there is first the difficulty of making the sounds of the *huruf*, the difficult letters in the back of the throat, like: *ayn*, where you grind a reluctant motor with your larynx, or *khaa*, where you scrape the bottom and top of your palate together, or *qaaf*, a thick clucking accomplished with much practice. Without getting into the mystical and religious significance of the Qur'an, let me just say that it is replete with marvellous examples of patterned and syncopated language of sublime beauty, and to be able to read a sura like Ar-rahman, The Merciful, in classical Arabic par excellence is well worth the trouble of learning the Arabic alphabet.

Both Heighton and Noyes elaborate on the benefits translating poetry has brought to their own writing lives. Heighton claims that:

The work of translation has made me a better poet because every translation I undertake is a kind of master class with a writer I admire. To approximate Rimbaud's notoriously difficult, hundred-line Symbolist masterpiece, "Le Bateau Ivre," I had to read the poem over and over, and live inside it on and off for months – and some stanzas I kept re-entering and studying and revising for over a year. By the end of the process, I not only felt that I'd learned a lot about the possibilities of poetry in French and the art of Rimbaud in particular, I'd also learned more about *English* poetry and my own practice; after all, I had to locate English approximations for Rimbaud's neologisms and bizarre imagery and surprising rhyme. I am fortunate in being able to translate whatever individual poem excites me, from whatever language or time period.

Noyes, while he admits that his knowledge of Chinese and Arabic can lead him to "sometimes writing poems that are obscure. Or they too easily bewitch me with their purloined sounds and I can't see that they don't signify for others the way they do for me," also suggests that such forms of "play" are vital for the poet as "the value of translation, among other linguistic practices, is that it provides different ways to enjoy language, and I believe that it contributes to the poet being able to come up with the right word with the right sound, shape and texture when they need it."

Toronto poet Beatriz Hausner has made translation an even more integrated part of her poetic practices. Here's how she answered my questions on why she started translating and what makes it so important:

**How did you start?**

I was in my early teens when my family moved to Canada from Chile. My stepdad, the poet and collage artist Ludwig Zeller, brought with him a scarce few books (from an immense collection), basically the poetry that nurtured and represented his poetic sensibility at the time. There were many Latin American poets of his generation and a little older in that cosmology. These he reinforced and complemented with readings of the Spanish classics, as well as French poets and German poets. He read to us in Spanish, and with me, seeing that I was interested in poetry, he discussed and he shared. Ludwig's world existed for me exclusively in Spanish. So I grew up with a keen understanding that there was a need to somehow transfer his knowledge, his world, his sensibility into the world that I was making for myself in English. The prevalent thought in my mind was: "wow, people my age, people like me who don't speak Spanish, should *know* these wonderful writers!" Being an immigrant child I always translated; in modest and very raw ways, I was always translating, perhaps not formally for publication, but practically, for the purpose of learning.

Later, when I was doing undergraduate studies in Spanish and French literature, I began to translate in a more purposeful and directed way. Mostly I translated the surrealist writers my parents published under their Canadian imprint, Oasis Publications. I began with an essay by the Argentine surrealist Aldo Pellegrini, a kind of philosophical premise about the true nature of the poetic, one which I embrace entirely, namely that poetry is about transforming reality.

I did a lot of translation all through my twenties and thirties, mostly the writers of Spanish American surrealism, although I also translated writers whose work is very different from theirs, including Canadian writers, whom I translated into Spanish.

**Why did you do this?**
In the beginning I translated out of a need to disseminate, to share all this fabulous literature with my peers in English. Now I only translate those writers and texts that most approximate my own writing and I do so as a means of truly entering the source text and making it poetry in the target language, in my case the language of my own poetic expression. In a very true sense I consider the translation work I do now to be a form of writing, not a mere transfer.

**What effect has it had on your own poetry?**
Translation has provided me with the best literary education possible. Beyond its influence on my process, however, the greatest excitement provided by translation has been the recognition of voices that are sister voices, modes of expression that at once mirror and refract my own, all the while enriching me, inspiring in me new ways of writing.

**Suggestions for those translating other poets?**
Translate only the *best* writers. There is too much left to be translated and the opportunities to publish are so scarce.

# Hosting a Radio Show and Running a Poetry Reading Series

*Poetry has agency in the world.*
– George Bowering, *Left Hook*

Over the years, I have been a guest on quite a few radio programs, from university radio to co-op shows to, once, the CBC, where a host interviewed me on my book *Cusp/detritus: an experiment in alleyways*, and told me to read my poems in a more monotone way while popping SweeTarts in his mouth. Being interviewed and reciting on radio can be nerve-racking as you can't see the audience and are concerned with keeping the flow of words going to avoid the peril of dead air. Yet, for the listener, hearing poems on the radio is almost a perfect experience, less distracting, more resonant. The mind can more readily concentrate on the sounds of the voice on the radio than either live or on TV or the computer. An impromptu energy often occurs between the host and their guests, like a game of lyrical Ping-Pong, engaging both the ear and the mind. At their best, radio shows nurture variety and freedom in art, encouraging experimentation and slipping beyond censorship. While I have never run a radio show myself, I have hosted, either co- or solo, a number of reading series since 1994.

I began with the Corner Pocket series, hosted by myself and Chad Norman in New Westminster, which invited a stellar range of guests including Al Purdy, Miriam Waddington, Marya Fiamengo, Russell Thornton, Patrick Lane, Peter Trower and even Anne Marriott, who by then was in a wheelchair after a stroke, I reading the poems she had selected while she nodded in rhythm. After this Norman and I ran other series: at a cafe called Myles of Beans; in Ernest Hekkanen's living room, where we also featured musicians and prose writers like Annabel Lyon; the Stone Room series at El Cocal restaurant; the Studio series on Pender Street (which ended abruptly after a soused Geoff Berner tossed his shoes through the nine-foot window) and one-time-only events at Café Deux Soleils presenting Joe Keithley from D.O.A. singing, Robert Priest reciting and artist Maurice Spira chalking a massive mural on black tarpaper. We also read poetry to seniors at Dogwood Lodge and hosted an event at the library – KNOW Canada – to introduce the public to early Canadian poets like F. R. Scott and E. Pauline Johnson. The year 2000 saw Norman, myself, Karen Moe and others working together to create Corazon, a performance salon in Moe's east-side apartment, which set up shows by Mecca Normal and readings by Joe Rosenblatt. In 2004, I hosted my first solo series – Placebo – at a little theatre off Commercial Drive in Vancouver. Again, I had musicians play prior to poets like Mike Schertzer, a collaborative environment I expanded further when I moved to Edmonton in 2006 and ran the 44th Avenue Troubadour series in my home for two and a half years, playing host not only to musicians and poets, but also fiction writers like Lynn Coady and photographers such as Paul Saturley, along with dancers, videographers and painters. I always commenced these evenings by reciting a poem from a tro-bairitz and ended them by serving wine and bowls of pretzels, dried fruit and yogourt-covered peanuts. I moved back to Vancouver in 2012, and Warren Dean Fulton and I ran The Living and the Dead at the Heritage Grill in New Westminster, featuring living poets like George Bowering and their deceased mentors, in the form of recitation, audio or video presentations and Fulton's immense collection of archived texts and materials.

Yes, poetry is an aural and oral art form, best appreciated when well crafted for the page and then brought to one kind of stage or another, whether a radio program or a reading series. When poetry is listened to without the distraction of the visual – as on a radio show, or in the presence of an appreciative, engaged audience – it becomes a more moving and entertaining creation. Although poetry was originally only a spoken art, after the invention of the printing press it eventually became mostly a written genre. Until 1949, when, as Stephen Kessler reminds us, "a poet and pacifist named Lewis Hill" created the first non-commercial radio station, KPFA in Berkeley, CA, a station that regularly featured poets reciting their work including Dylan Thomas in 1952 and 1953. One of the most innovative programs on this station was 1975's *Calling All Poets* in which listeners phoned in to recite poetry on air.

During the 1950s, the American poet Cid Corman also started to experiment with what he called oral poetry. In 1952, this act involved spontaneously composing poems into a tape recorder and then afterwards hosting a broadcast called *This is Poetry*, in his belief that: "radio is [the poet's] best potential outlet [as it] puts the stress rightly on the spoken word [and] tests the imagination." Allen Ginsberg expanded this practice in the 1960s by undertaking readings regularly on the radio and, subsequently, poet David Antin, who had heard some of Corman's tapes and shows, began composing his "talk poems" by improvising in front of an audience: creating "a hybrid of criticism, poetry, and storytelling. [Then he would] tape record the pieces," which could end up on a radio show or even in a book. The poets of the beat generation had a particular emphasis on performance, creating events that merged poetry with jazz and chanting. Since then, despite what seems like dwindling poetry book sales, poetry performance venues continue to increase, especially in the spoken word or slam community, but also for more page-based poetry for the poet who wishes to read locally or go on a cross-country tour.

Radio shows that feature poetry in Canada are mostly located in colleges and universities. The CBC, however, has featured interviews with poets since its chat with E.J. Pratt in 1958 on the occasion of his seventy-fifth birthday. The station also held the CBC Poetry Face-Off in 2009, which offered spoken word poets the chance to compete for prizes. Vincent Tinguely, in an overview of co-op radio programs for LitLive.ca, wrote about how radio and even TV has cycled between celebrating poetry in shows like Lillian Allen's 2004 CBC radio show *Wordbeat*, MuchMusic's *Word Up!* and Bravo's *Heart of a Poet* series, and sending it underground again, which Tinguely claims has been its fate since about 2007. Along with Joe Blades and

R C Weslowski, Tinguely spoke with the recently deceased radio host Nik Beat, whose show *HOWL* ran for at least twenty years and with Penn Kemp who hosted *Gathering Voices* on the London, ON, station CHRW FM, the latter emphasizing that "concentrating on the voice in radio rather than gesture or physical presence in communicating poetry has taught me to listen acutely."

Reading series are much more diverse in their venues than radio shows. They can be run in cafés, bars, libraries and bookstores or even, usually as one-time events, in bakeries, aquariums, train stations or public parks. The Bohemian Embassy, run by Don Cullen in Toronto, was the first poetry and music performance series in Canada (run at 7 St. Nicholas Street [1960–66], then at Rochdale College [1970], Harbourfront [1974–76] and finally Queen Street [1991–92]) with Le Hibou in Ottawa coming next, run by Harry Howeth from 1960 to 1975. Today, the Art Bar Poetry Series is the longest-running poetry-only series (1991–present), run out of different bars and restaurants (currently at the Black Swan Tavern) with an ever-changing roster of hosts. There are pop-up reading events in every city in Canada and all major cities have their own series, from ephemeral ones like Weslowski's Under the Bed in Vancouver to established ones like the Pivot Reading Series or Hot-Sauced Words, both in Toronto. Of course, major cities and some smaller ones also host writer's festivals, from more grassroots endeavours like the Whitehorse Poetry Festival to now firmly established, corporate-sponsored multi-genre annual events such as Calgary's Wordfest or the Vancouver Writers Fest.

While most bars will let you host a poetry series if you bring along a drinking crowd, it's usually a bit harder to get on the radio. However, most colleges and universities have a radio station that is open-minded and into the possibility of letting poets host radio shows, often in connection with presses or performance series.

Here is Ontario-based poet Bruce Kauffman on running a radio show:

I launched a reading series here, in Kingston, ON, at the Artel, about three years ago . . . I wanted to create something that might inspire others as I had been inspired. As I realized the talent and desire within this reading group month after month, I knew they deserved a bigger audience and I approached CFRC 101.9 FM with a program idea and a demo. Exactly one year after the poetry open mic reading series was launched, *finding a voice*, my radio show, was aired for the first time.

There are probably nearly as many ways to run a spoken word radio show as there are hosts running spoken word radio shows. I came into my own show feeling a bit techno-challenged and a little naive. I think it's important to admit and acknowledge your own weakness – and to be open – to growth, but more importantly to change. The radio show itself was built around the open mic at the Artel, and with it an unknown and uncertain mix of readings each week – mostly a mix from me reading from another writer's books. When I quickly realized this wasn't sustainable for a weekly one hour show, I made a decision then to begin to include monthly on-air interview / readings with local poets – which grew into both local and not so local poets / authors, and as often as the desire or the need arose – and then, to recording other local events.

S. R. Duncan, a Vancouver poet and radio personality, co-hosted *Wax Poetic*, a weekly half-hour spoken word show, from the studios of Co-op Radio, CFRO 102.7 FM (now 100.5 FM) in Vancouver, BC, from 1998 to 2010. The show was founded by Justin McGrail and Diane Laloge in the mid-nineties and was first called *A Way With Words*. After Duncan, R C Weslowski was asked to come on board to share the technical and administrative responsibilities. It is Vancouver's longest-running poetry show.

Duncan discusses why he became a host:

Doing *Wax Poetic* combined two big joys in my life: present-day spoken word and old-time radio plays – which are likely what inspired me to start writing in the first place. Poetry and radio naturally complement one other. Radio is a great medium for poetry.

In Canada, apart from the CBC, the only types of traditional broadcast radio stations receptive to regular spoken word/poetry programming are college/university and co-operative ones. The big plus to this kind of amateur radio environment is how we are much freer to bring on whoever we want – to talk about whatever we want. While you can occasionally get away with that on commercial radio, your job is always on the line when you do, and generally speaking the owner of the station and the advertisers wield control over your destiny and career.

That said, co-operative radio is also run by a collective of very strong-minded, passionate and sometimes downright militant individuals. In reality, only a small handful of people really envision and influence policy in most non-profit organizations. Clashes of opinion can and will happen regularly, but heads seldom roll. Although we are never able to pay our guests (as is par for radio), they do end up with a quality studio recording of the interview, plus potentially unlimited exposure on the Internet. I believe this fills a real need for many guests who don't have a lot of exposure, maybe not even a website. If the guest is registered with SOCAN [Society of Composers, Authors and Music Publishers of Canada], however, they will receive royalties. The occasional writer also receives travel funding from the League of Canadian Poets, in part from appearances on our show.

Perhaps the biggest benefit to doing the show, for me, is how I felt immersed in the literary culture locally, nationally and even internationally. We always give priority to people with upcoming events, and have been invited to many over the years, big and small. The tickets and swag we got was always fun, too. And we got to give away a ton of stuff! Randy [Jacobs, a.k.a. R C Weslowski], my co-host, has a deep relationship with the slam family, which brought us many great spoken word performers from all over North America. Keeping our format loose allowed us to meet and talk to so many different creative types, not just poets, but musicians and visual artists, too. The wisdom and inspiration I've gained is priceless.

My time on the show has given me a lot of insight into how media works and I've tried to put it to good use in my publicity and performance career.

Another radio show host and poet is Montreal-based Jeffrey Mackie. Starting, in the 1990s, on the same Co-op Radio program in Vancouver that S. R. Duncan hosted, Mackie then worked at the radio station CKUT in Montreal as an evening arts show host before being asked to undertake the morning program. "The major component of the show I produce," Mackie explains, "has been me inviting authors on the show to be interviewed and to read from their work. Though I get suggestions sent to me I usually choose which writers I would like to have on. I attend many events and awards shows and so meet and hear a lot of authors." Over the years, he has enjoyed many memorable moments discussing the craft of writing on air. He also likes "having the poets read on the radio and being able to spread poetry around a little more in our world." For him, "running the show has personally enlarged the writing community and exposed [him] to different forms and approaches when it comes to writing poetry." He asserts that as poetry is an oral art form, and feels that if you appreciate the public reading of literature then initiating a radio program is "an essential starting point." Mackie suggests the novice host talk to their "community station as they have a mandate to serve their neighbourhood and hire people who can give you training in the various aspects of radio production." Take the initiative, he encourages, and see what evolves in the innovative world of poetry on the radio.

While radio shows focus on interviewing their guests along with giving them a chance to recite, reading series generally stick to the performance itself, perhaps also offering a question-and-answer period afterwards, as the Lunch Poems series at Simon Fraser University (SFU) currently does. Only one reading series I know of, called "An Evening With" at the now-defunct Aqua Books in Winnipeg, engaged in on-stage interviews with its invited poets.

Garry Thomas Morse, one of the poets I spoke with who hosted, or "preambled" as he calls it, a performance series, talks about his event:

> The Kranky Reading Series featured Vancouver poets and writers on the first Thursday of every month. It was a thrilling May to December "romance" in 2011, with dynamic readers trying out a fair amount of concentrated and experimental material. I would say that this series offered something to the community at large, and that the audience in attendance was always different, depending on the writers being featured. Perhaps it was for that handful among the public who want to hear excellent readings without feeling obliged to purchase something or to align themselves with the viewpoints of a given group. And when I was at the Kranky Cafe, it was my best chance to put aside all my authorial and promotional activities and to listen for one hour to three excellent writers, and naturally, that informs my work more than any other.

A much more long-term series host is Victoria poet Wendy Morton who hosted Mocambo Poetry Reading Series and Planet Earth Poetry for ten years from 1999 to 2009, when it was then taken over by Yvonne Blomer. A series involves a fair amount of both work and foresight. As Blomer explains:

[Running a series] involves being on the ball most days and having both a long-term vision of the coming year, and a week-by-week idea of who is coming and what those poets need as far as funding, accommodation, pick up, dinner and other details. The biggest job is the Canada Council for the Arts grant application done each February for the March 1 deadline, followed by a reshuffling of poets when the grant comes in. Then I do applications for reading tour funds through The Writers' Union [of Canada] and League of Canadian Poets. The next big job is making sure there is an audience each week – fortunately, we are fairly established in our location now and have a pretty dedicated following of over thirty people each week. I'm always trying to boost these numbers through university, college, community and collaborative events.

Both Blomer and Morton enthuse about the positive impact running a regular series has on their poetry. For the former, "the poems and conversations about poetry" that she is a part of each week inspire her "to keep up the more solitary path of writing"; while for the latter, the series became "one of the highlights" of her week. Morton looked forward to the "delights of the night," ranging from the "singing, dancing poems" themselves to the joy of seeing inexperienced poets gain the confidence required to perform. However, as gratifying as running a weekly series is, Blomer cautions, "Don't do it every week. Especially when you start, start with once a month and see how that goes. If you are in a smaller community, try four to six times a year. I would also suggest collaborating with a literary journal, a university or college, or another venue for in-creased support."

Another experienced host, Joe Blades, a poet from Fredericton, NB, has been part of running many literary reading series over the past fifteen plus years. Some of these have been as a solo host, as with the River Reading Series at Molly's Coffee House; others have been as part of a collective, such as the annual International Multicultural-Multilingual Poetry Reading event he organizes and hosts along with Nela Rio. He has also hosted reading nights for the League of Canadian Poets and the local poetry radio show in Fredericton called *Ashes, Paper & Beans*. He continues to host series because it benefits the community and because he's "good at it," he says, so, "he keeps being asked!" Running poetry events also helps his own writing, as he elaborates: "Hearing writers read their work is often stimulating to my creativity. Kernels of inspiration: mus-ings, leaping-off points . . . all occur in the stimulation of hearing writers perform their creations. Working with writers and other event organizers builds community and opportunity both locally and for my own reading aspirations elsewhere. Readings are a great way to get feedback on what I am writing – especially new writing. Readings enable me to give my writing to those whom Ted Hughes calls its 'co-authors.'"

Taylor Leedahl, a younger poet from Saskatchewan, now living in Montreal, discusses her more recent experiences with running a reading series at greater length:

I launched Tonight it's Poetry (TiP), Saskatoon's only weekly poetry series, in April 2008. Saskatoon didn't have a poetry series and my poetry debut, *No Apologies for the Weather*, was coming out that fall – no good! At the time I was working for Thistledown Press as the marketing person and had gained some valuable skills (and confidence) in organizing literary events and was making connections in the national literary scene. As a total freshy in the professional writing scene, I was looking for people who were around the same age as me and/or also early in their writing careers. I knew there were other young writers out there (I took many writing workshops in my youth) but didn't have contact with them. TiP kind of started out as a call to young writers.

Saskatoon already had a poetry community, but it was pretty scattered and small. I know this because my mom, Shelley A. Leedahl, is an author, so I was introduced to book launches and poetry readings at an early age. I'm big on respect, so I knew it was important to somehow include the existing community (locally and nationally) and that the emerging writers would benefit from this inclusion. Ultimately, TiP became an intersection between established and emerging writers. Each week four emerging poets would have seven minutes on the mic (the Community Stage) and one featured poet would present their work for half an hour. TiP nights started out as mixers: emerging writers met one another and started to grow as a community. The featured poets were local or from elsewhere in Canada. Often they would approach emerging writers whose work they really liked or even mentioned the writers in their own set.

TiP began in this little bar called FLINT in downtown Saskatoon. Within a year we outgrew the venue when the audience grew to forty to fifty regularly. People often had to stand. One night we had Lorna Crozier as our featured poet. Professors from the University of Saskatchewan came down for the show and complained that the venue was too small. I had to smile. For quite a while I hung on to that venue and just packed it . . . made people stand for poetry. It felt so great!

My friend Charles Hamilton moved back to Saskatoon from Victoria, BC, and I asked him to start a slam series within TiP. Those nights, the last Sunday of the month, really took off. People loved to compete and they loved the spoken word artists we featured. The first poetry slam final we had was so packed that people watched from the street. There was an outdoor speaker that was connected to the PA system and the front window was an overhead door that opened up like a garage. One person parked their car in front of FLINT and sat in the trunk with their friends to watch the competition! We went another half season in at FLINT, but it became too crowded so we moved to a much larger venue on Broadway called Lydia's.

In 2010, I decided to continue with my academic career and got into Concordia University (Montreal) to write my M.A. in art history. I directed the series until the end of the 2010 season and handed TiP over to the collective. I appointed Charles as the director and the other members, Lisa Johnson and Stephen Rutherford, took on more rigorous roles. TiP has since just kept growing. The collective is doing an amazing job. It's common for there to be one hundred to one hundred fifty at each show . . . I think there's been as many as two hundred fifty. We're even hosting the Canadian Festival of Spoken Word, the national poetry slam competition, next year.

Bonnie Nish, from Vancouver, has been running Pandora's Collective for many years, a group that hosts the Twisted Poets' Literary Salon and the Annual Summer Dreams Literary Arts Festival. When asked how undertaking both crucial ventures have impacted her own writing she replies enthusiastically: "Doing this year after year has been good for me. Keeping me in the loop with other writers and what they were doing helped me to grow as an artist. It allowed me to open up and explore in ways I may not have." When she first began the series and then the collective and festival, it was easy to get overwhelmed. She recalls that "the best bit of advice anyone ever gave me when starting a reading series was to give it at least six months to a year to take off. Don't get frustrated. These things just take time to grow and reach an audience."

Whether it's a radio show or a live poetry series, such community-based initiatives are crucial. They boost performance confidence, increase the diversity of the scene and serve as a network of aural nerve endings that stretch across this immense country, binding artists together through public presentations of their work.

# Running a Small Press

*I see all of my work in the context of community.*
– Gary Barwin, interview with the author

Before 1993, I never thought about small press publishing. When I was a teenager, if I dreamed about my work being published it was in magazines or else by the big presses. In fact, when I was seventeen years old I submitted a children's story I had written to the large press Douglas & McIntyre and was confused by their rejection, knowing nothing about what they published, or what the submission process was. After taking a writing workshop with Patrick Lane in '93, where he told me to "do it yourself," I started my small press called Wet Sickle. Of course, I didn't actually own a press so mostly what I did was typeset the text, select the paper and get an artist to design the cover, then take the book to a printer. From 1993 to 1996, Wet Sickle produced two of my chapbooks, two of Chad Norman's, one by the Stray Dog Poetry Project (a reading group that Norman and I belonged to) and one by Gloria Barkley, with her poems about living in the tiny town of Hedley, BC. Then I ran out of funds and didn't take up small press publishing again until, living with Warren Dean Fulton, we ran Above and Beyond Productions in 2012–13, producing a calendar of Vancouver poets, a broadside and a few chapbooks, including one by Joe Rosenblatt.

As a poet, I have published my work with many kinds of presses both trade and chapbook. Chapbooks have emerged as photocopied and stapled productions from above/ground press, as collaborations with an artist from JackPine Press and as one-of-a-kind art books from Red Nettle Press, crafted with twine, leaves and sticks for binding. My first non-self-published chapbook was released in 1999 by Mecca Normal's Get to the Point Publishing and featured a black die-cut vinyl cover revealing red text beneath. Attending events like *Broken Pencil's* zine fair or running a small press book table at Word on the Street has opened my eyes to the immensity of possible creations, the vitality of poetry as an experimental genre and the benefit poets can reap by remaining close to DIY culture.

In North America, there is a lengthy tradition of poets serving their literary communities by starting magazines, chapbook presses or, more recently, running e-zines or blog sites. Certain schools of poetry rose to prominence almost entirely on the strength of their small press publications. As Michael Hayward states in "Unspeakable Visions: The Beat Generation and the Bohemian Dialectic," a paper written on the history of the beat generation:

For many of the Beat writers, publication in these little magazines marked their first appearance in print....

Often run on a shoestring budget, and lacking the reputation of the more established literary magazines, the underground magazines were labours of love for the people who published them. In many cases they represented the only outlets for poets just starting out, those yet to acquire a name for themselves. . . .

Each magazine was its editor's voice, and these numerous, varied voices were used for the exchange of ideas throughout the underground.

In the book *A Secret Location on the Lower East Side: Adventures in Writing, 1960–1980,* Steve Clay and Rodney Phillips discuss how the emergence of the small press movement occurred: "Direct access to mimeograph machines, letterpress, and inexpensive offset made these publishing ventures possible, putting the means of production in the hands of the poet. In a very real sense, almost anyone could become a publisher. For the price of a few reams of paper and a handful of stencils, a poet could produce, by mimeograph, a magazine or booklet in a small edition over the course of several days." Today, of course, the process has become increasingly digitized but many small presses still take the handmade route to publishing.

In Canada, according to Gregory Betts in his discussion of "The Rise of the Small Press Movement in Canada" from the website Historical Perspectives on Canadian Publishing, "the models of publishing and dissemination developed by early small pressers, especially through such little magazines as *Contemporary Verse, First Statement,* and *Preview* from the 1940s, were imitated and developed by dozens of magazines in the 1960s and 1970s through to the present," thus emphasizing the influential nature of the small press journal's origins. Along with magazines, such presses as blewoint-ment emerged, run by poet bill bissett, and Very Stone House, established by poets Patrick Lane and Seymour Mayne. Betts continues:

> Similarly, the role of the publisher becomes indistinguish-able from the role of the artist. bissett, with his blewoint-mentpress (founded in 1963), and bpNichol, with Ganglia Press (which he started with David Aylward in 1965), intentionally blurred the borders between art and life. Using whatever technology was at their disposal, they published experimental and eccentric writing in experimental and eccentric book objects: some books were stapled, others folded, others sewn, and others perfect-bound; some were handwritten, others typed, rubberstamped, or printed us-ing Letraset (transferable lettering). The physical labour in-volved and the thoughtfulness and beauty of each literary object remain a hallmark of the small press movement....
>
> Many projects by early experimental small pressers left the conventionally-defined book behind altogether.

Significantly, Betts points to the fact that while some authors are more interested in producing chapbooks or appearing in zines at the beginning of their publishing vocations, he believes, "others pre-fer the aesthetic freedom and marginal 'outsider' cultural position of the small press." Retaining such a sense of freedom as a poet, detached from commercial or academic ends is, I believe, vital to the flourishing of the art form.

Former poet laureate George Bowering also discusses the de-velopment of the small press in Canada in his book *Left Hook: A*

*Sideways Look at Canadian Writing*. Focusing on the Montreal-based Véhicule Press, he points out how, early on, even the trade book attended to artistic elements, inspired by chapbook production and presentation. For instance, Ken Norris' book *Vegetables* was released with a seed packet stuck to the front jacket that you could actually plant! Those involved in the trade press also created other kinds of publications, as with Stephen Morrissey's magazine *Montreal Journal of Poetics* or John McAuley's more experimental Maker Press. Unique to Canadian publishing is Coach House Books, begun in Toronto in 1965 by a young typesetter named Stan Bevington. Coach House published such key texts as bpNichol's *Journeying & The Returns* and Michael Ondaatje's *The Dainty Monsters*, but its originality also resides in how it has always maintained a dual role in Canadian letters by both publishing and printing books. Whether individually or collectively, Canadian poets and publishers have created an energetic burgeoning of small presses and magazines from the 1960s until today.

Upon speaking to five contemporary small press publisher-poets, I found the ideological and aesthetic approach to cultural freedom Betts mentions to be very much the case. Mark McCawley, who has published the zine *Urban Graffiti* for eighteen years, first in paper format and most recently online, comments on the types of writing he can publish in his zine that don't usually appear in most traditional Canadian literary journals: "Transgressive, discursive, post-realist writing concerned with the struggles of hard-edged urban living, alternative lifestyles, deviant culture – presented in their most raw and unpretentious form." The market for such work, he suggests, is limited: "For the longest while, the only markets for urban post-realism have been *Urban Graffiti* and Matthew Firth's *Front & Centre* magazine. The addition of *The Puritan* and *The Loose Canon* are hopeful signs."

Small press publishers must often make this trade-off; they have greater freedom to publish the material they personally support but often, their audience base is minimal. "Originally above/ground press (founded in 1993) came out of an awareness that small publishing existed in other places, other times, but there didn't seem to be anything going on at all in the city of Ottawa," explains long-term small press publisher rob mclennan. Along with producing chapbooks, broadsides and other ephemera, he also published *STANZAS*, a magazine that was a direct response to George Bowering's long poem magazine *Imago* (1964–74). mclennan "managed some forty-six or forty-seven issues before the whole thing fell apart, distributing hundreds of copies of each issue gratis." As he claims, publishing a small journal was both altruistic, in that he wanted "to provide a space for the long poem to exist in print, in pre-trade collections," and self-motivated in that he desired to shape a venue for himself to "exist as a reader and writer" of this particular form.

Stuart Ross, who now lives in Cobourg, ON, is one of the best-known small press creators and aficionados in Canada. "My life has pretty much been devoted to the small press world," Ross begins by saying. Starting with the publication of his own work in 1979 by "photocopying a twelve-page, unstapled collection of my poems, in an edition of fifty copies, on the photocopier in my dad's office," Ross quickly caught the small press bug and started publishing others with this company he had dubbed Proper Tales Press. In 1982, he began producing chapbooks and postcards and broadsides by poets such as Mark Laba, Lillian Necakov and Michael Boyce. The press is still running, releasing work by poets as diverse as Canadian Paul Vermeersch and American Ron Padgett. Ross has also produced a range of literary zines, his longest running being *Mondo Hunkamooga:*

*A Journal of Small Press Stuff,* "which began in 1982 and went for about twenty-three issues." He has also run a poem blog called *The Week Shall Inherit the Verse.* On top of all this activity, Ross was also "the co-organizer of the first three Toronto Small Press Book Fairs, beginning in 1987, and before that, with Nicholas Power, the co-organizer of the monthly Meet the Presses event, a gathering of small press publishers that ran throughout 1985." Further, since 2007, he has run his own small press–style imprint under Mansfield Press.

John Pass, who lives in Madeira Park, BC, has run High Ground Press with his wife, writer Theresa Kishkan, since the 1980s, printing their exquisite broadside series of poems and artworks on a Chandler & Price platen press built in the 1880s. Pass not only loves the freedom he has to select whatever authors he chooses to print but also the sensory pleasures of operating a tangible letter press. He describes: "the physicality of letterpress printing: smelling the ink, hearing the stiff swish/slur of its gradual spread under the rollers on the inking disc, touching each sheet of paper as it's fed to the press, pedalling the beast, hearing and feeling in the pedal the subtle clunk in the mechanics of impression, scanning the copies as they're taken off and reaching to place them gently to dry in rows on an adjacent table. The dance-like, trance-like rhythm of all that going on at once ... is poetry to me."

When I asked how publishing a magazine or running a small press contributes to their own writing practice, all five of the poet-publishers were effusive, Ross perhaps most so. He asserts: "I think it's a good practice: to publish oneself and publish others. Every writer should have that experience. I also believe that small presses are a home for things that wouldn't otherwise be published. Small presses are where just about everything interesting happens."

Humorously, he concludes, "If I were the King of Poetry, I would make it mandatory."

More briefly, rob mclennan notes that being a publisher has made him increasingly "formally adventurous" and has enlarged his attention span for "longer projects," while Trisia Eddy, who ran Red Nettle Press out of Edmonton, admits that although publishing took up many hours she could have used on her own writing projects, when she returned to her own work, she found that the time she spent creating chapbooks made her "newly inspired." Mark McCawley, meanwhile, enthuses on how being the editor and producer of his zine has increased his ability to "experiment with his own writing," thus serving as a "liberating" force in taking his creative work in new and thrilling directions. John Pass feels that printing broadsides is partially motivated for him "by the altruistic notion of giving something back to the world of literature, to writers and writing" he admires and that this exchange invariably serves his own writing well too.

Unlike with the big presses, whose imprints can seem amorphous and with corporate intent, the small presses usually present a defined voice and presence. While chapbook publishing is completely devoid of an economic motive as the presses are usually funded out-of-pocket and sales are often minuscule, small presses are more frequently government funded but continue to present a quixotic and rich array of authors, released from the demand to sell thousands of copies of a particular title. While some, like Biblioasis in Windsor, are concerned to publish local names, others, like BookThug in Toronto, have a definite stylistic brand that appeals to a certain kind of writer. Running a small press, whether a chapbook or trade one, can allow a poet to trumpet their tastes and place their mark on a generation of texts, thereby contributing to Canadian literary history.

# Mixing Mediums

*There comes a point when an hour of sketching objects from life or learning to play an instrument will make you a better writer than another hour of writing or reading will.*
– Steven Heighton, *Workbook*


When I was younger, and for many years into my commitment to writing poetry, I felt a certain level of possibly healthy fear that, if I failed to immerse myself in depth with my primary art form and instead took up writing a novel or trying to paint or play the flute, I would weaken my bond to the poem. That it might, like a snubbed child, turn from me. I did, of course, dabble in private with such art forms as collage and plucking a guitar from time to time, but resisted making anything other than poetry public. One, I sensed I wasn't "good enough" and two, felt perhaps that to show one's work at all requires a total commitment to its particular form. I worried that to offer less than this would be a profound insult to others who had dedicated their lives to the art. By the time I had been solely writing poetry for about ten years, though, I felt confident enough, or maybe even restless enough, to start experimenting with other art forms publically. I learned to play the bass guitar and to sing, and participated in the creation of several metal bands. I took photographs and occasionally exhibited them. I acted in two solo theatrical productions, one in New York in 2008, at the Sage Theater. And I engaged in collaborative work with other visual artists, creating both websites and multimedia exhibits. But why is there this apparently marked distinction, and its created tension, between the writer and the artist?

In an article in *The Atlantic*, William Deresiewicz explains how, from 1767 on

art disentangled itself from craft . . .

"Art" became a unitary concept, incorporating music, theater, and literature as well as the visual arts, but also, in a sense, distinct from each, a kind of higher essence available for philosophical speculation and cultural veneration.

Thus, one angle on this separation of writer from artist is that writers may still be hovering between clinging to craft on one hand and spiritual mysticism on the other. Additionally, while the word *artist* may give one a picture closer to the reality of a painter, sculptor or videographer, it doesn't provide much specificity when considering what a writer does. Writing has always seemed, and is, more of an inner and solitary activity than the more externalized, physical and sometimes collaborative nature of art. Possibly this explains the uneasiness a writer can feel leaping those bounds.

Deresiewicz elaborates: "Under all three of the old models, an artist was someone who did one thing – who trained intensively in one discipline, one tradition, one set of tools, and who worked to develop one artistic identity. You were a writer, or a painter, or a choreographer. It is hard to think of very many figures who achieved distinction in more than one genre – fiction and poetry, say – let alone in more than one art. Few even attempted the latter (Gertrude Stein admonished Picasso for trying to write poems), and almost never with any success." Under the much bandied about ten-thousand-hour rule, any artist is supposed to sink themselves into one art form and never "deviate" from that path. However, not only is this singular model of the "solitary genius" becoming less popular, or perhaps even less feasible, given the massive amount of stimuli the contemporary artist is exposed to, but today, likely, "technique or expertise is not the point. The point is versatility."

Regardless of definition, the desire to mix mediums entails the poet taking up another art form in which to explore their creative engagement with the world, whether it's with paints, movement, the camera, clay or an instrument. Many poets create in mediums other than words. They may have talent in multiple medium forms; they may also seek simply to explore alternate mediums from an urge for diverse self-expression or to inhabit the materials and visions that other mediums utilize and inspire. Whether someone is particularly gifted as a painter, sculptor, dancer or musician, learning how to mix colours, carve wood, move to rhythms or play an instrument can only add to their appreciation for art, expand their skill set and perhaps even result in the formation of a band or the organization of an exhibition.

Now-deceased American poet Stanley Kunitz once described how his work as an amateur sculptor affects his creation of poems:

"My hands want to make forms. Though my poems often deal with the time sense, I'm inclined to translate that into metaphors of space. I like to define my perimeters. I want to know where a poem is happening, its ground, its footing, how much room I have to move in." The South African poet Pitika Ntuli also utilizes his sculptural abilities to enhance his poetry, combining his poems with his artwork, learning to carve and patinate verses directly onto his hot metal creations.

Rita Dove, a former US poet laureate, draws her inspirations for poetry from her other love, dance, stating passionately:

Poetry is a kind of dance already. Technically, there's the play of contemporary speech against the bass-line of the iambic, but there's also the expression of desire that is continually restrained by the limits of the page, the breath, the very architecture of the language – just as dance is limited by the capabilities of our physical bodies as well as by gravity. A dancer toils in order to skim the surface of the floor, she develops muscles most of us don't even know we have; but the goal is to appear weightless. A poet struggles to render into words that which is unsayable – the ineffable, that which is deeper than language – in the hopes that whatever words make the final cut will, in turn, strike the reader speechless. ("Poet at the Dance: Rita Dove in Conversation")

In terms of painting, as the educator Harry Rusche addresses, an association has been made between this art form and poetry since "the Roman poet Horace set down in his *Ars Poetica* (c. 13 BC) the dictum 'ut pictura poesis' – 'as is painting, so is poetry.'" Ernest

Hemingway, who wrote highly poetic prose, once remarked that at times a writer could obtain information about perception and scenery by observing an oil on canvas, or even making one, in ways one might not gain when reading another author's prose, admitting, "I learn as much from painters how to write as from writers."

Musically speaking there are even more connections to poetry. Peter Saint-Andre, in "The Individualism of the Poet-Musician," discusses the history of poet-musicians, elaborating how such musical poetry "first appeared in ancient Greece with Archilochus, Sappho, and Alkaios (poets who accompanied themselves on the lyre, thus the designation lyric poetry)." Then, in the eleventh to thirteenth centuries, first the Goliards in Europe and then the troubadours in Southern France played musical instruments to accompany their recitations. Leonard Cohen, contemporary Canadian poet and singer, talked with Jeffrey Brown on *PBS NewsHour* about the distinctions and connections between writing lyrics and composing poems:

> JEFFREY BROWN: What's the difference for you between writing a poem and a song?
> LEONARD COHEN: A poem has – a different time. For instance, a poem is a very private experience, and it doesn't have a driving tempo. In other words, you know, you can go back and forward; you can come back; you can linger. You know, it's a completely different time reference.
>
> Whereas a song, you know, you've got a tempo. You know, you've got something that is moving swiftly. You can't stop it, you know? And it's designed to move swiftly from, you know, mouth to mouth, heart to heart, where a

poem really speaks to something that has no time and that is – it's a completely different perception.

JEFFREY BROWN: It's interesting, because poetry – often we hear poetry is about music, in a sense, as well. Poetry makes its own music, sometimes it's said.

LEONARD COHEN: Oh, I'm not saying it's not musical; it's just a different tempo. And it's a tempo that migrates, depending on what the mood of the reader is.

Cohen's thoughts on the connections between poetry and music, especially in terms of them possessing differing tempos, underscores a further validity of practicing additional art forms – it enables you to better comprehend one medium through the lens or score of another. In such a way, ideally, the creation of each medium is strengthened, as can be the case when a writer learns more than one language.

In speaking to Canadian poets about their involvements in a range of art forms, I discovered both an eagerness to define oneself as an artist regardless of medium and a desire to discuss how the secondary art form complements what they consider their primary art form, poetry. Joe Rosenblatt, who lives on the west coast of BC, and has been a poet and a painter for over forty years, describes the merging of both media: "My poetry and the visual arts nourish each other. There is a cross-fertilization of ideas. As a result of this reciprocal process the two disciplines conjoin as one. I make no distinction between creating visual art and writing poetry; for me, painting and drawing are just other ways of writing poetry."

And indeed, in his work, the preoccupations of both art forms in terms of subject matter are similar; as he puts it, "birds, cats, bees and fauna." However, each approach highlights different aspects of his obsessions; the writing is more surreal, the painting is more fanciful; both mediums serving to find variant ways of fleshing out his relationship to the universe.

Another poet, Shawna Lemay from Edmonton, also uses the visual arts to expand her depth of involvement in making her poetry. "My daily practice includes taking photographs," she explains, and this ritual has enabled her to "find the poetry in the everyday." Most importantly, she asserts that photography, while being a source of beauty in itself, is also a way to feed her poetry as "the more creative you are, the more creative you are." Lemay expands on this vital process: "When I was mainly concentrating on my writing, I needed some container for the overflow, and this is what led me to taking pictures nearly daily. Also, when I'm stuck in my writing, I've often found that picking up the camera is what gets me unstuck. I can't imagine not having photography as part of my writing practice anymore, so integral is it to my creative stance."

Paul Vermeersch, Toronto poet, speaks from the position of having started as a visual artist and then deciding to give up this practice for fifteen years to focus on poetry. In 2013, realizing that combining the two art forms could provide a fruitful release, he picked it up again. I asked him four questions about the importance of the visual arts for him in relation to his work as a poet:

CATHERINE OWEN: When did you start making visual art?
PAUL VERMEERSCH: I can't remember a time when I didn't enjoy painting and drawing. It seems I spent my entire childhood doing it. When I entered university, I studied visual art as well as literature, and I focused on painting

98/ The Other 23 & a Half Hours

and drawing. I even showed some pieces in galleries here and there. So you see, it's hard to say exactly when I started making visual art. But I can tell you when I stopped making visual art.

When I was twenty-three I moved to Poland to take up a teaching position at a college there. My intention was to paint in my spare time. I hoped to paint enough to have a solo exhibition when I came back to Canada. In the end, I only made three or four paintings in Poland, but I came back with about two hundred pages of poetry – pretty rough stuff, but it was the basis for my first book. It was around that time, the end of the 1990s, that I decided I needed to focus my energies on one art form if I was to make anything of it, and I chose writing. I put my paint brushes away and my first book came out in 2000.

I started painting and drawing again in a meaningful way toward the end of 2013. A year or so earlier I found a trove of art supplies at a yard sale, and I bought the lot. Still, I needed a push. In November of 2013, an old friend contacted me. He owns an old painting of mine from the '90s, and he was asking to purchase another one. A commission to make a new painting was just the nudge I needed, and I've been at it with a fervour ever since. After all, I have fifteen years of not painting to make up for.

CATHERINE OWEN: How does it converse with your poetry?
PAUL VERMEERSCH: I think I was right to stop painting to focus on writing when I did. I needed to focus on one thing at the time, and I'm very happy with how my writing has evolved, and how it continues to evolve, but things

are different now. Making art no longer competes for my mental energy in the same way that it used to. If anything, painting is a way for me to recharge. Writing for me is mentally taxing, but painting is relaxing, even meditative. Between teaching and editing and reading and writing, I can get overloaded with language fairly easily, but painting lets me catch my breath while engaging a different part of my brain. I think it's good for me, and I think it has been good for my writing, too.

CATHERINE OWEN: Why do you (if you do) think it's important for poets to engage in mixed media work too?

PAUL VERMEERSCH: I can only speak for myself, because every creative person has their own relationship to their creative process. For a long time, I didn't work in multiple media. I wrote poems and that was it. If there's a benefit to painting in addition to writing, beyond the mental recharging I've already mentioned, I'm only just discovering it. I assume there are many benefits, in the same way that an athlete who cross-trains sees holistic benefits.

CATHERINE OWEN: Are there any drawbacks to this practice?

PAUL VERMEERSCH: The main drawback that I can see is time. There's never enough of it. It's hard enough to find the time to pursue one art form, let alone two. But somehow, I find it. The time, that is. The work gets done because it has to get done.

Along similar lines, a prime example of an integrated creative stance is the Torontonian poet and musician Robert Priest, who has played guitar and sung for years, and worked with other musicians to record his songs and bring them to the stage. While I initially encountered Robert as a poet, very soon I realized he is a musician too and that his poetry and songs often stem from similar places. He is equally charismatic and engaged in connecting to his audiences when performing either kind of art.

Priest explains:

I write songs, poems and videos (both poetic and rock-based) with collaborators. I started writing songs with collaborators in high school in the '60s. I would write lyrics and my friend Michael Manuel would write music. I also had a rock band in the late '70s early '80s called the Defayds and I wrote a lot of songs with Eric Rosser where I supplied a lyric and he put it to music. This then morphed into a children's repertoire which we put out under the band name the Boinks. In the '80s I wrote a lot of songs with a lot of people including Nancy Simmonds, Alannah Myles, The Jitters, Gwen Swick, Neil Chapman and notably Allen Booth, with whom I still write.

When asked how this practice has contributed to the development of his poetry, Priest comments that while his musical work hasn't contributed much to his adult poetry,

it has contributed to the rhythms and templates I use for my children's poems and song lyrics, all of which typically use rhymes and metre. Here it has tightened up my sense of rhythm so that I've gone from a fairly loose sense of

verse to a more exacting one. Often when I co-write with
Allen Booth, if he gets some good music happening on a
particular verse I might then compose new verses based on
that music, so it has brought more discipline to my verse
style. In fact, I regard the writing of song lyrics as an inte-
gral part of poetry. But when you do it you realize that all
the bogus attempted constraints on modern poetry, such as
that it shouldn't be romantic or contain a polemic, cannot
possibly hold in the song form. This can be enlightening
or frustrating depending on how obedient you are to cur-
rent fads in poetics. (I advise disobedience or, if it's not too
late, complete ignorance of all such poetics.) Once you've
begun to work in this medium it's a matter of following
your own tastes and adapting and containing your own pre-
dilections in the spirit of compromise, which the meeting
of music and poetry often requires of both the composer
and lyricist. This can be refreshing when posited against the
typically hermetic solo approach most of us take toward
writing poetry. It can bring a sense of community and pro-
duce art that is possibly attractive to various performers,
which can thereby take on a life beyond books or one's own
performances.

Since the year 2000, another BC poet, Wayde Compton, has
worked off and on, alone and with artist Jason de Coutu to create
turntable poetry. He describes his process in an essay from his book
*After Canaan*: "In various venues, including classrooms, art galler-
ies, and nightclubs, and with either choreographed or improvised
sets, I have conducted live audio mixes of pre-recorded hip hop,

jazz, spoken word, and dub plate [or one-off] recordings of my own poetry." Through this fusion of poetry with music and technology, Compton writes that his relationship with his art has altered in positive ways. Within these performances, he has transformed his poems into "art object[s]" that exist in a space outside of his own body and have reconfigured the primary nature of the poem for him, turning it, in its dub plate recordings, into "one source among many," enlarging the nature of authorship to include the auditory and collaborative, and enlarging the act of writing by enabling it to communicate through mixed media samplings, music and recitation.

Other artists use video to bring poetry to a larger, often more diverse public. Here poets use cameras to capture their poems along with visual imagery; they then post the completed pieces on YouTube or submit them to various videopoetry competitions and festivals. Sometimes the poets learn the technology themselves; others, if they have a budget or willing volunteers, work with videographers to create the finished product. The initiator of videopoetry in Canada, Tom Konyves, states, "Video allows poets to see their work more clearly... in video we substitute visual lines for printed lines and proceed to 'layer' a poem." As Edmontonian poet Kath MacLean adds, making video poetry is creative "in a very different way than writing. It's more like theatre – I've only done one play, but loved it. That was loads of work (and expense) and this is too, but since video poems are short it's more manageable." Heather Haley, who lives on Bowen Island in BC and has long been known for both her work in fusing music and poetry and running the Visible Verse Festival, a celebration of the art of the videopoem, expands on the history of the medium and her motivations for undertaking the latter multimedia experiment:

I believe Jean Cocteau was the first poet to employ film. In 1930 he produced *The Blood of a Poet*, usually categorized as surrealist art. Then there were the "film poets" from the West Coast abstract school, James Broughton, Sidney Peterson and Hy Hirsh, the latter two collaborating with John Cage in 1947. In 1978 Tom Konyves of Montreal's Vehicule Poets coined the term *videopoetry*, to describe his multimedia work. Rather than get bogged down in semantics, I'd like to point out that I think in terms of moving images, and don't make a huge distinction between film and video. I work with digital video because it is accessible and affordable, important considerations for most poets. I'm drawn to video because of its populist nature. It lends itself to hybridization and its history of experimentation is a fundamental aspect of the medium. Video is a natural fit for me, having grown up with television and cinema.

However, Haley, unlike Rosenblatt, emphasizes that, despite her achievements in music and film, "I view myself as a poet. Sometimes I choose to disseminate my work via video or by fusing it with music. But my practice is writing poetry."

Other poets aren't even concerned with bringing the other mediums they participate in to the stage or a gallery; instead, they undertake these additional art forms as ways of exercising other senses and interacting with the world a different way. Poet Jane Mellor uses dance to deepen her ability to connect with "the meditation of creative work, the focus that is required."

Along with the exercise that dancing provides her, vital as a contrast to the largely sedentary work of writing poetry, dance also echoes the rhythms of her writing practice: "I've discovered how dance really helps with the movement of my work – of my words. My poetry tends to be very musical. It carries a lot of rhythm. Dance is obviously poetry of the body and it inspires the words I write. I get just as lost in my dance practice as I do in my writing practice. I'm not always aware of it but sometimes when I reread a piece I am aware of how it was inspired by dance, how I've transferred the poetry of dance into the poetry of verse."

All these writers possess a sense of fearlessness in relation to their willingness to create other forms of art without worrying about such inessential parameters as the ten-thousand-hour rule. They see art as feeding art, whether professionally created or engaged in on an amateur basis. Employing mixed media forms as an extension of writing or as a way of exploring other talents is evidently neither going to quash the sacred muse nor entail that one has less dedication to a primary art form. Instead, it can spark a flame beneath the desire to live life as an entirely committed maker of art in general, whether it's in words or clay or song.

# Collaborating

*Collaboration is key; it takes innovation and creativity to the next room.*
– Shawn Lukas

The romantic myth of the solitary artist, slaving away in poverty-stricken yet noble isolation, is a tenacious one. As with the fear of incorporating mixed media work into one's practices, a resistance to collaboration is unfortunately common. The writer can become anxious about an invasion of their creative privacy, about their boundaries being pushed or about who receives credit for the final creation. And these can indeed all be risks. But the flip side is the chance to meld your mind with another's, enter a different kind of mysterious process of energy generation and rise beyond the self into a project that may very well transform your notions of creativity.

Among the bands, theatrical work and multimedia installations with other visual artists that I have done, I found the riskiest collaboration I undertook as a writer was co-authoring a collection of sonnets, called *Dog*, with renowned Canadian poet and painter Joe Rosenblatt. Over the course of four years we sent octets and sestets zinging back and forth via email to each other, all the while we both had to be respectful to each other's process and to listen carefully to each other's voices with the aim of having them echo rather than meld. In the end, we also had to be willing to detach ourselves from our egos when it came to selecting the best possible pieces for our collection. The risk was in the time and energy put into an experiment that, in the end, could have failed, and in being willing to let many of one's personal modes of composition fall by the wayside in order to allow for another mode of writing. Collaborating in this way not only let me forge a deeper friendship with Joe, it helped me hone essential aspects of my poetic craft.

Collaborating with other artists can be viewed almost akin to work in other art forms, especially in the case of such artistic acts as creating videopoems, where the line is thin between how much of the multimedia work the poet is making herself and how much she is collaborating on with a team. Often poets will not play instruments themselves or dance or paint, but they will recite with a band or be backed by dancers or have a painter be inspired by their poem and create visual art based on their words. A poet can write with another poet, composing a piece together, whether it's a form poem like the *renga* (a style of collaborative poetry originating from Japan) or a sequence of narrative pieces that each riff off similar subject matter. Of course, poets can also take poems that have already been written and compose new pieces based on lines or images from these poems. Finally, poets can work with other poets in creating performances emphasizing the aural qualities of language or creating elaborate soundscapes, as with the composition of librettos or with groups like The Four Horsemen (a collective that started in 1970 comprised of members bpNichol, Rafael Barreto-Rivera, Paul Dutton and Steve McCaffery).

Although North American poets haven't historically been eager to collaborate with each other, perhaps due to geographical distances or a greater emphasis on the individual nature of authorship, poets in other countries have long traditions of collaborative composition. For instance, in Japan, many haiku poets write linked or collaborative poetry, such as *renku* and *tan-renga*. In these poetic forms, two or more poets are required to compose alternating stanzas. Such collaborative forms not only require communication between the involved poets, but they also entail a level of respect for the communal practice. Not only is the piece written together with others but these participants must be equally involved in determining what occurs to the final work in terms of performance and publication.

While collaboratively composed work isn't common in North America, Canadian sound poetry groups such as The Four Horsemen aimed to create aural poems dependent on each participant's full involvement. As bpNichol once said, the works "are formed by four individual voices but it is that moment of group identity that we have striven for." Contemporary American poets Denise Duhamel and Maureen Seaton have been writing poetry together for fifteen years, a partnership that has resulted in three books, some of them influenced by the random practices of surrealist art. As Duhamel expands, "we've written Exquisite Corpse sonnets, sestinas, pantoums and villanelles. We've even written Exquisite Corpse centos, which are made up entirely of lines from other poets." As they live at a distance from each other that precludes regular meetings in person, they have used everything from the answering machine to email to enable their collaborations, getting together when possible to engage in more elaborate writing exercises.

In the US, the Black Mountain poets, like Charles Olson, Robert Creeley and Gary Snyder, were famed for working with musicians and artists to create fascinating bodies of multimedia art. Creeley, as one example, not only worked with visual artists, such as Jim Dine, Alex Katz and Susan Rothenberg, lending his words to their paintings, but he also released albums where he recited to the accompaniment of jazz musicians like the trio Forever Sharp and Vivid, and jazz bassist and composer Steve Swallow. As he once noted, "to me the timing that I use, or depend upon, in poetry is very, very, very like the timing that they are using variously in music and especially jazz or bebop." Lyn Hejinian, an American poet, has additionally collaborated widely with artists such as Emilie Clark. Poet C. D. Wright, in an interview for *Jacket* magazine, also discusses the collaborating she has accomplished over the years, describing how she started working with other artists after becoming "bored with [her] solo act." In Wright's case, the artist she co-created projects with was the photographer Deborah Luster. Wright started by composing a "long, twisted erotic poem" while Luster incorporated Wright's piece into her photos, utilizing a French technique, "mordancage"; later work has involved poetry imprinted on metal, upon which photos of prisoners are engraved. Speaking generally about the challenges and joys of collaborating, Wright admits that the "very bone of collaborating [is] a willingness to make mistakes. After all, no one is in total control. One is always attempting to say or see something through the other one's mouth or eyes. And since this is impossible, mistakes are made." Collaboration between artists is definitely becoming a more popular practice, testifying to the rich possibilities of drawing ideas, rhythms, imagery or even just energy from another's artistic storehouse. Collaborating with another artist or poet also diminishes a writer's sense of isolation and can open up more venues and audiences for these co-creations.

The Canadian poets I interviewed tended to be enthusiastic about collaborating with other artists or fellow writers, even though financial support is hard to obtain for such projects. Heather Haley, videopoem creator, also talked to me about her desire to work collaboratively with musicians to create another entrance point for poetry, a further audience for the art form she loves: "Music can be a powerful vehicle. It's entirely possible to find and develop a rapport with a guitarist, cellist, accordion or banjo player – according to your own bent – to accompany you and your words. In my *AURAL Heather* work, which I call 'spoken word song,' I collaborate with musicians in several ways. They might compose melody to accompany my words, or I will write poetry to go with their music, improvising and experimenting along the way, a 'fusion' of spoken word and song our goal."

Although Haley admits that it is "difficult because music is a collaborative process, requiring compatible collaborators, and it also requires resources," when the multimedia experiment succeeds it is even more satisfying than working solo, perhaps because it is so challenging to engage with the limitations and capacities of other art forms, and as the end result tends to reach viewers or listeners who might otherwise be resistant to poetry on its own.

Angela Rawlings, who writes and performs as a.rawlings, has been engaged over the past ten years in a wide range of collaborative efforts. Often these entail turning her poems into sound and movement performances, with musicians and video artists. Her performance called *Environment Canada*, for instance, was largely developed with Belgian vocal artist and opera director Maja Jantar, while her piece *Drift* began when musician Nilan Perera approached her with an idea for text improvisation. They had "several sessions," Rawlings recalled,

> where we'd work with his drift technique, noting discoveries . . . our approach was to launch headfirst into working with text with only the bare-bones structure in place. Corporeal mime Julie Lassonde joined us and we continued to work in this way of "do first, discuss after." In both collaboration and performance, this has very much been a practice of having to generate absolute trust in my choices, in the choices of my fellow collaborators, and in the rewarding risks available in improvisation. I consider the work that I do to be interdisciplinary in nature. I'm interested in bodies, and how bodies experience sound, text and movement.

Rachel Rose from Vancouver wrote in a solitary fashion for decades before being commissioned to write a libretto with composer Leslie Uyeda, in 2011. This was performed as an opera in the summer of 2013. In an interview on the *Lemon Hound* blog, she states,

> Collaborating has been interesting and mostly quite joyful. I know some poets who have felt that the composer used their words as kind of a salad, picking out the choice bits and rearranging them on their plate as they saw fit. My experience was the opposite. The composer a poet longs for knows poetry, knows how to read it, appreciates and

respects the words as the scaffold, the bones of the body of music. I have rarely felt this kind of deep attention, and I would wish that every poet feels this at least once in her career: it's better than ten years of therapy.

Through the auspices of the Internet, and particularly with the appearance of social networking communities, more poets appear to be collaborating on texts with multiple authors. Gregory Betts, a poet from Ontario, began the Three Words Per Poem project on Facebook, using the medium to "harvest lyric poetry for creative purposes," as he describes it. Drawing on an initial text, he posted three-word chunks from it and asked readers to "finish this sentence." As the foundational text was three hundred words, one hundred comment streams eventually opened up, thereby engaging a range of different kinds of poets in response: "over two hundred people contributed over 2,300 alternative endings – the largest poetic collaboration ever," Betts concludes the interview with. He then edited the comments slightly, and ended up with a tidy, funny and smart collection of one hundred collaboratively crafted poems.

Taking a more politicized approach to collaboration, Christine Leclerc from Vancouver, BC, has fused her socially conscious passions with her writing and used the Internet to create the Enpipe Line project. She elaborates on its beginnings and what it aims to achieve:

On November 1, 2010, The Enpipe Line project was launched in Prince George, British Columbia – a city along the proposed pipeline route. Poet and professor Rob Budde read about the Enbridge office occupation in July, and, noting that I taught creative writing at the University of British Columbia, invited me (and poet Reg Johanson) to read at the University of Northern British Columbia. Both Rob and Reg have contributed poetry to The Enpipe Line.

A call for submissions went out over the Internet and contributions started to arrive from poets the world over. I started to measure the poems, and post on my personal website, though the project was later moved to its own site at http://enpipeline.org [now defunct]. The long poem [that resulted] is comprised of the poems submitted to The Enpipe Line website in resistance to the proposed pipelines, and stands in solidarity with similar projects that resist social or environmental destruction. While the initial goal was to collect 1,173 kilometres over a two-year period, The Enpipe Line grew to over fifty thousand kilometres in less than one year.

Poems submitted to The Enpipe Line were hand measured. If they were not submitted in 12 point Times New Roman they were put into this font. The poems were then hand measured in centimetres. Sometimes we used handmade rulers. Next the poem lengths were converted from centimetres to kilometres to reflect the fact that The Enpipe Line's actual height is one kilometre. Why so big? Because the height of the text is intended to match the width of the right of way requested by Enbridge to build their proposed pipelines.

The Enpipe Line's poems come from people who fight Northern Gateway [Pipelines] in their communities. They come from people ready to move toward renewable

energy and away from fossil fuels. They come from some of
the world's finest poets. They come from people who have
never written poetry in their lives. The Enpipe Line's con-
tributors are of all ages and from all walks of life.

Several of the collaborators with Leclerc – also Vancouver poets,
namely Jen Currin, Jordan Hall, Ray Hsu, and Nikki Reimer – add
to the details of the Enbridge Pipeline project with their own com-
munal perception of what collaboration can be like for artists:

My collaboration is like orange slices held in place by
other slices . . . I am never bored collaborating. Into the
shared skull of a thought I might have had, but didn't. My
collaborator(s) did. Already I am uncertain who wrote
these words. I collaborate to visit mind pantries and to
share mine, across the cubicles and beneath floors that feel
comforting. To mark out a field and play a secret game, to
play at lawyer and architect and demolitions expert. And
blanket forts. And forge upstream. Grab a comrade's raft
and float back down. What is poetry? Am I flexing? Are we
flexing in a row? Are we holding hands? Can we do this in
time to the music? We have strung up these lines together
and now watch them glow like Christmas lights. Each illu-
minated bead: a reminder. You all. Remind me. That writing
is never alone.

Susan McCaslin has also spearheaded a collaboration called the
Han Shan Poetry Project in a successful attempt to preserve a for-
est in Langley, BC. She describes how: "Two hundred poets from

British Columbia, across Canada and around the world submitted tree poems. We suspended them in plastic page protectors in the forest for two months over Christmas. People came from far and wide to stroll and read poetry. The story garnered coverage in the *Globe and Mail* and *Global News* and the forest was eventually spared. This collaboration, she asserts, "not only effected political action, but showed how powerful it can be when poets work together with an essential aim in mind."

Prior to the development of social networks, email was the first truly valuable tool for more immediate long-distance projects. Douglas Barbour, an Edmonton poet, using email, forged a collaborative relationship with the American poet Sheila E. Murphy, in order to write a book called *Continuations*, a project that took ten years to complete. Barbour, in his introduction to the book, puts their work into the context of similar attempts by Canadian poets to merge their voices to create a multi-textured piece, such as the group Pain Not Bread, formed in 1990 by Roo Borson, Kim Maltman, and Andy Patton. [Also] Anne Szumigalski & Terrence Heath's *Journey/Journée* (rdc press), *Negative* by Daphne Marlatt and Betsy Warland and the collaborative writing group known as Yoko's Dogs. Pain not Bread, for instance, not only melds the voices of the three poets (Borson, Maltman and Patton), but also hearkens back to the ancient Chinese poets they have studied and honour in the compilation, *Introduction to the Introduction to Wang Wei*, a book also ten years in the making.

Sheila E. Murphy, in an interview for *Jacket* magazine on her work with Barbour, provides a more encompassing commentary on the nature of collaboration, stating that: "Collaborative writing offers an extraordinary element in creative partnership that concurrently teaches and crafts a manuscript of dual making. This craft demands the writers to be both attentive and inventive." Barbour also feels that collaborating has made him more prolific as a poet, and enthuses that "the process of jointly writing an extended piece naturally entails risk, but the sustained engagement associated with the crafting of what is possible in language easily surpasses such risk. Stabilizing structural features such as the six-line format and daily practice provide the necessary structure for propelling innovation" (interview).

Stuart Ross, who we heard from earlier on the pleasures of running a small press, is also likely the most prolific and adventurous artistic collaborator in Canadian poetry. In his compelling book *Our Days in Vaudeville*, where he co-writes poems with twenty-nine other poets, Stuart provides an introduction to his collaborative history and its importance to his creative life. He emphasizes how "collaborating is absorbing because you're constantly reacting to someone else's text. . . . That is the sublime beauty of collaboration: you're implicated in something you couldn't possibly have written alone." This is an assertion the poems – composed in a range of methods from word by word to thematically, and by every means from email to in person – attest to.

Poets can even collaborate with authors in books, taking inspiration and material from other writers' poems to compose their own in a more unilateral form of collaboration. Poets such as Shane Rhodes, Ken Babstock, Catherine Graham and Paul Vermeersch have worked with lines from other writers, whether prose or poetry, dead or alive, utilizing the words as a springboard for their poems, to address or politicize the texts or, as with Graham, to find a way to interweave the tones and concerns of two poets in the creation of seamless new pieces. Another poet, Barbara Hunt, has written a whole book whose poems leap off lines and images from well-known poets' works. She explains how "collaborating in this way has taken me in new and unexpected directions in my art. Think of following the voices of Billy Collins compared to Sharon Olds, Roo Borson or Margaret Avison (from whom I really learned to mash up word images!). The past three years using the technique of riffing off other talented poets (not always, but often) has strengthened my poetic voice, cultivated the texture of my poems and keeps my work ever-evolving beyond just my own experiences."

The possibilities of collaboration with a range of varied artists are truly endless.

# Engage with the World

## Travel

*The world is a book and those who do not travel read only one page.*
– Saint Augustine

Travel can be local or international; random or planned; intentional
or mysterious. Regardless of whether it's a bus trip around town
or a hike through the Himalayas, writers have long benefited from
stepping outside their comfort zones in relation to direction, lan-
guage, levels of endurance and other kinds of risk. I have usually
interspersed periods of isolation or "roosting" with jaunts into
unfamiliar territories, almost always with a manuscript in mind, al-
though the end result is often very different than my initial vision.
The two primary trips I have taken for my art have been to France
and Turkey in 2007 and to Mexico in 2011. On the former journey,

I wanted to obtain a deeper understanding of troubadour culture by connecting my textual research with a tangible experience of the land, while the latter sojourn sought to meld my reading of Malcolm Lowry's novel *Under the Volcano* with an observation of the rituals surrounding the Day of the Dead. While I rarely travel in "unscripted" fashion because I have never seen much of a point in sheer relaxation without the undercurrent of a project, such a trip could help writers to detach from their daily routines and release them from levels of stress that may be restricting their creative process. However, when travelling in cultures distinctly different from your own, writers should remain aware of the issue of cultural appropriation. As James O. Young and Susan Haley point out in their article, "Nothing Comes from Nowhere: Reflections on Cultural Appropriation as the Representation of Other Cultures," artists can engage in the appropriation of a culture when they represent these others in ways that may not be sensitive to their context and thus can capitalize on unequal power relations. Of course, there are always ways to enter another culture respectfully and without usurping the voices of its inhabitants.

In relation to the positive effect travel can have on writers who are attentive to their surroundings, John Tranter enthuses: "You get a surge of energy, a jolt of understanding, and a marvellous change of perspective when you first encounter a civilisation totally different to your own. It really opens your eyes in a way that no amount of reading, or movies, or television, ever can." Jonah Lehrer, in an article called "Why we Travel," even states that "jumping on a plane will not only make you smarter, but more open-minded and creative." Fortunately, one doesn't even have to go that far to benefit from the influence of travel. Ross Hudgens, building on Lehrer's point, claims it is "the neurological transfer of the familiar to the unfamiliar" that remains influential. Which means you could even take transit into a different part of town or go for a walk within a previously unexplored landscape or even remain in "the comfort of [your] own home" and reap similar benefits. Writer Michael Mewshaw puts it in even more vivid terms: "Travel for me is a kind of writing, an alternate text, a preliminary draft. . . . It is an act of creativity in which the world is an empty page and I'm the pen scrawling looping, recursive lines across a landscape. . . . It's my method, a la Arthur Rimbaud, of systematically deranging my senses, opening myself up to the new and unexpected."

Historically speaking, the medieval troubadours are perhaps the most renowned poets who travelled for their art. They toured from town to town in Southern France, drawing inspiration from the landscape and performing their work in the places they stayed. Sometimes, of course, their travel was necessitated by persecution and exile, but regardless of intent, leaving their homelands and sojourning to other locales gave their poetry a new source for engagement with the world. Walt Whitman, nineteenth-century poet of the self, also travelled extensively across North America, as described on the Library of Congress website: "In 1879 Whitman traveled to the Great Plains and the Rockies. He exulted in the panoramic and sublime landscapes and wrote about the experience from St. Louis. . . . In 1880 he toured Canada with his close confidante Dr. Richard Maurice Bucke." His poem, "Song of the Open Road," details his beliefs in the value of the "road" and how it encourages the freedom of thought through which poetry emerges:

O public road! I say back, I am not afraid to leave you –
  yet I love you;
You express me better than I can express myself;
You shall be more to me than my poem.


Whitman was a strong adherent of the practice of leaving one's home and wandering in the world; roaming without a necessary itinerary and remaining open to the influences one encounters in unfamiliar environments, from unique dialects to alternate landscapes. Later, in the mid-twentieth century, the group of poets and writers known as the beat generation took this philosophy to fascinating extremes. From Jack Kerouac's famed novel *On the Road* to much of Allen Ginsberg's poetry, travel was a core theme and obsession of these writers. Ginsberg, for instance, travelled in his lifetime to East Africa, Mexico, India and China, among other places.

His poetry was filtered through what he learned in these countries, from Buddhist philosophies to political activism. Additionally, in the later part of the twentieth century, Raymond Carver, the American poet and short story writer, wrote poems about Europe and Buenos Aires and even street fairs in Mexico. And as for Canada, now-deceased poet P. K. Page travelled and lived in Brazil in the later 1950s while Gwendolyn MacEwen, who died in 1987, travelled to the Middle East in 1962 and even lived in Greece for a number of years in the 1970s, her travels producing books like *The T. E. Lawrence Poems*. Although it has seemed in the twenty-first century that travel is influencing fewer poems, perhaps due to the exorbitant costs of taking planes or trains or to the fear that writing poems about other cultures can be viewed as a form of colonial appropriation, there remain poets who travel on a regular basis and see such adventuring as a major source of essential fuel for their art.

Four poets I talked to, all but one from Alberta, travel regularly and view such trips as stimulating material for their poetry. Kimmy Beach, whose home base is in Red Deer, describes two different kinds of valuable travel. One is impromptu, such as when she was "a teenager backpacking across Europe . . . and keeping an incredibly detailed journal." She hadn't planned to write on the trip, but found herself needing to detail all her experiences, raw material she later drew from to write a book of poems. The other kind of travel is planned in relation to a specific project, as when Beach returned to Liverpool to research her collection *fake Paul* about The Beatles. She believes that travelling in order to collect subject matter for a book helps the poet avoid factual errors and increase sensory and historical viability. Any poet, she claims, who aims to have fun and experience a sense of freedom while they research should travel, reminding us that there "must be joy in the practice of writing – and I would add in the practice of research – even if the subject is not joyous itself."

Jannie Edwards, who emigrated with her family from South Africa to Alberta when she was six years old, states: "Travel is irrevocably tied to adventure in the family mythology I inherited, in which my parents were both risk-taking wanderers. My dad, in 1932, signed on to the merchant marines and worked for his passage from London to New York City, to take one story, and both my parents kayaked down the Mosel and Rhine in 1935." Since she's retired from teaching, much of her travel has been on the road, through the States and into Mexico. She and her husband of forty plus years live in a trailer with their dog for however many months their sojourn takes them. Edwards explains how "the forced confinement of long stretches of driving, where the landscape settles into your psyche – well, this produces a state of reverie, of daydream, of waking meditation. It frees up the mind." Travel invariably loosens the grip that daily worries can have on the brain, and it gives you the time and energy to encounter characters that you might pass by at home. Edwards expands on an example of this opportunity: "Sometimes I carry these stories for decades before they make their way into my work. Like the sad-sack Caucasian guy we met in San Francisco in 1974 who had gone AWOL on three marriages/families and was living under the radar, earning dollars reading tourists' palms on Fisherman's Wharf . . . thirty years later he turned up as a character in the 'Debt Tango' in my book, *Blood Opera: The Raven Tango Poems*."

Patrick M. Pilarski from Edmonton has also travelled widely. Here's his trajectory of sojourning in his own words:

Over the course of my artistic career, I've been fortunate to travel widely and frequently. This travel has given rise to what I would consider some of my most original (and also most widely published) work to date. My favourite places for creative inspiration include an odd handful of extremes, including Iceland, Japan and the Antarctic Peninsula. Some travel takes me close to home; some takes me to the raw ends of the earth. Does my literary output from these voyages take the form of verbatim travel logs? My notebooks would suggest a unanimous negative. But for some reason travel has led to the most vivid, uncommon and downright abstract literary moments I've been lucky enough to put to page.

What turns travel into a fountain of ideas? I keep coming back to the following possibility: a journey forces (or seduces) the writer into living fully within the present moment. Perhaps the stream of new experiences, concepts and/or languages collides with a writer's preconceptions to sharpen their pen. Perhaps this same stream of highly salient stimuli washes away the ruts of routine, leaving a writer room (or free license) to experiment with something new. Perhaps it's just our old-school savannah mind, riveting us to the here and now.

Here's my best guess. I think it all comes down to not knowing what will happen next – travel induces a wholesale failure to predict the future. Our brain throws open its perceptual dragnet. Ideas that would normally drift by unnoticed in the current get hauled en masse (flopping and odorous) onto the shore. This has both metaphorical and neurobiological roots; you can take your pick....

.... Whatever the cause, travel continues to be one of my principal sources for inspiration. Even when I'm not explicitly writing about travel, travel is writing about things in me."

Gary Geddes, a poet who now makes his home on Thetis Island, BC, has travelled extensively throughout his life, and lists the countries he has explored as: China, Indonesia, Hong Kong, the Philippines, India, Thailand, Greece, Ireland, England, Scotland, Wales, Germany, the Netherlands, Israel, Palestine, Mexico, Nicaragua, Honduras, Costa Rica, Guatemala, Chile, Brazil and a number of countries in Africa. His ability to travel, he freely admits, has been made possible by his relatively comfortable life as an academic, which has given him both funds and time to make such excursions, as well as the unfortunately now defunct Arts Abroad and International Canadian Studies program that offered writers grants to travel as poets to other countries. But more important than these sources, is Geddes' belief that travel is an essential way to immerse oneself "in that more troubled stream, live cheaply, stick [your] neck out, take some risks, and try to understand at the grassroots level what is happening in more troubled places." He does not travel for relaxation or comfort, but to deeply unsettle his perceptions and routine. As he elaborates, he is "always overawed by the spectacle of cultures so different from [his] own and by the simple tasks of finding a cheap bed and reliable food or picking up useful phrases of the language." He firmly believes that "the self in stasis needs a regular shaking up, to avoid complacency, egotism and all the perils of thinking one's own lot is somehow the template for humanity."

Geddes adds that:

All writing . . . is mediated and subjective. . . . I try to be careful with the stories people share with me, asking permission, altering details, dates or names slightly if necessary to protect privacy, conscious of not betraying a confidence. Chinese, Spanish, Japanese, Israeli, American or Canadian history belongs to everyone. And, thankfully, we get to see ourselves through the eyes of others when they write about us. If we're smart, we don't fret about them asking permission, writing our story or "getting it right." There is no one right version of us. Instead, we rejoice in their interest, in the story that has been constructed, how insightful it is about events, psychology, and how well the language is being used, at the increased complexity of the tapestry that is us in this world.

Finally, Geddes states, more generally, "Living feeds the writing, so the fullest life, whether active or meditative, which includes family, friends, reading, work and whatever else can be crammed into the few short years we have, ought to produce our best writing."

As Alice Major underlines, in her book *Intersecting Sects*, it is not that poets "must do exotic things or travel to exotic places" but that they need "a kind of interpenetrability with the larger world to write works that will engage with an audience." Writing grounded in travel can be a tricky proposition, given the ease with which one can slip into cultural appropriation or be charged with it, regardless of how aware one aims to be. There is also the risk that so many boundaries can be shaken up that a period of creative silence can ensue. Yet, enlarging one's boundaries through exposure to a variety of languages, rituals and histories cannot help but enable one, with sensitivity and reflection, to become a more engaged writer.

# Free-Range Writers

*The arts will begin to wither if they are pulled too far away from funda-*
*mentals of how people really should and have had to live, over millennia.*
– Gary Snyder, "The Real Work (excerpts from an interview)"

Where is art best created and where does it belong? These questions
have no simple answer but they continue to reside at the core of
what it means to be an artist in the twenty-first century. A tension
has long existed between what is considered high or difficult and
low or accessible art. In Canada this schism is represented by such
"alternate" awards for writers as the Acorn-Plantos Award for Peo-
ple's Poetry (in contrast to establishment prizes like the Governor
General's Literary Awards) and the formation of such peripheral
groups as the Vancouver Industrial Writers Union (in contrast to
the well-known League of Canadian Poets). It is also represented by
those poets who work within what is still called the establishment

and those who choose or who are relegated to being outsiders of one kind or another.

Unfortunately perhaps, in this era, poets and teachers have become nearly synonymous in the public mind. In my life, while I have done some teaching, I have decided not to commit myself to academic employment for a range of reasons: fewer and fewer jobs with little security or income and the sense that I need a wider diversity of employment and experience. Thus, I have worked more consistently as an editor, along with undertaking such jobs as selling ads for a tattoo magazine and, more recently, working as a production assistant on TV shows like *Arrow*, along with films such as *Godzilla*. The fact that writers have always pursued other sources of employment has been increasingly dismissed and invalidated. In an article for NPR *Books*, David Orr reveals that "in the 2012 edition of *The Best American Poetry*, for instance, almost all of the 75 contributors have taught poetry in universities or earned an advanced degree in poetry, or (more frequently) both." Such an emphasis on similar goals, employment-wise, can lead to the homogeneousness of creation, "an interchangeability," according to Raymond P. Hammond, that results in "mediocrity." In other words, Hammond argues, poetry produced from within a system that rewards certain kinds of writing and that shapes a particular type of poet. As Charles Bukowski said in his letters, most people forget that "poetry can be written by a bus driver, a field hand or a fry cook." While working blue-collar jobs or non-institutional jobs is far from a necessity for an artist, being employed as a professor certainly shouldn't be viewed as a primary goal. "The new paradigm," as William Deresiewicz stated in his article in *The Atlantic*, involves people holding "five or six jobs, in five or six fields, during the course of their working life," leading the career trajectory of the "multiplatform, entrepreneurial artist [to] be more vagrant and less cumulative."

Robert Phillips puts this issue into perspective, commenting how, in the past, most poets held jobs that one could consider outside their comfort zone. As examples, he offers "Chaucer was a clerk of the King's Works. . . . Donne and Swift were deans of churches. . . . Stephen Crane was a war correspondent, and Edwin A. Robinson worked in a customs house. . . . Robert Frost was a poultry farmer. . . . Hart Crane packed candy in his father's warehouse, worked in a printshop, wrote advertising copy, was a riveter in a Lake Erie shipyard, and finally managed a tea-room." He also cites the more well-known cases of the Modernist poets: "William Carlos Williams was a pediatrician, T. S. Eliot a banker, and Wallace Stevens a vice president of an insurance company and an expert on the bond market." They had jobs that didn't recognize their literary abilities and provided them a relatively protected academic or intellectual space in which to function. In terms of early Canadian poets, E. J. Pratt was originally a minister; F. R. Scott, a lawyer; Charles Sangster, a clerk and newspaper editor; and Al Purdy and Milton Acorn both worked blue-collar jobs for much of their formative years. Today, however, more poets are likely to hold teaching positions after obtaining either an M.F.A. or a Ph.D.

Yet there are many other possibilities. Dana Gioia, who worked for General Foods as an advertising executive, discussed his decision to work in a business environment in a 2007 interview with Michael Useem, stating that "there is a natural connectivity, at least in American culture between the creative and the commercial." He claims that the level of talent in the business world is high and that being around such stimulating, ambitious people has provided fuel for his art. Barbara Jane Reyes, a Filipino American poet, is another contemporary writer who chooses not to teach for a living. She says proudly, "I am one of those writers whom many of you would consider as holding a day job, when in fact, my day job in public health I consider my career. It's beneficial to the work of writing to have a life and perspective mostly outside of academic circles." Sina Queyras, on the Poetry Foundation's *Harriet* blog, interviewed Canadian and American poets who work in jobs outside of academe and found that none of them would trade their positions for a scholarly one. Dani Couture from Toronto works for non-profit organizations, Brad Cran of Vancouver is a tax accountant, New Yorker Gary Sullivan is the managing editor of publications at the National MS Society and fellow American Michael Kelleher is an artistic director. The majority of them describe their jobs as offering them more freedom to pursue their art, a better income, more job stability and a deeper connection with the wider world.

Ron Charach, who has practiced as a psychiatrist in Toronto for decades, asserts that pursuing an atypical career for a writer has held multiple benefits for his art. He states:

Two clear sources of poetic inspiration were medical school and working as a psychiatrist. There was plenty of drama, what with the gross anatomy lab, pathology labs and the occasional life-and-death situation bursting through, at the least expected times. There were many people to get to know up close, teachers, colleagues, patients, and that most challenging group, psychiatric patients, many of whom provided windows on who I really was as a person. Like many poets, I began with a hungry eye, and the usual traits of voyeurism and exhibitionism. But psychiatry provided plenty of training for the ear, that most bisexual of organs, which both passively takes in, yet actively obtrudes. Listening closely to so many varieties of people telling unimaginable tales of heroism and woe, sometimes like a fortified armadillo, at other times, like a desert fox, not only improved my ear for dialogue, for how people *really* talk, but enlarged my perspective.

He added that not only practicing psychiatry, but absorbing the theories and literature associated with his profession proved to be influential.

Reading, or attempting to read psychoanalytic texts was very dreamy, and nudged my writing in a more surreal direction, but the classic physician writers like William Osler, [Sigmund] Freud, Oliver Sacks, Anton Chekhov and William Carlos Williams persuaded me to portray people and things in a descriptive way, in the very way that they presented themselves. At the age of sixty-three, after about thirty-four years of inviting people to unfurl their lives and accept occasional feedback and measured advice, I still find the shadow world of psychiatric anamnesis as intriguing as the fictive worlds of the poem and the novel. And being on the receiving end of so much confession, how can I not take time out, in my own work, to confess?

Sandy Shreve, a poet who now lives on Pender Island, BC, worked for many years as a library assistant, then a secretary at

Simon Fraser University, followed by a final stint in legal aid, ending up each time in middle management. When asked how this work affected her creation of poems she replies:

> Initially my day jobs blended well with my writing life, as I was part of the work-writing movement and both the job and union activism inspired many of my poems. I was lucky that my jobs put me in environments where I was exposed to several of my interests (literature, feminism, justice) and to people who were willing to share their expertise in these areas. As well, I think being in the workforce . . . [enabled] a bit of distance from the intensity of writing and studying poetry, the insularity of sitting at my desk fussing over words. It gave me connections to other people, other lives and experiences I would not have otherwise come across.

She does concede, however, that if one is a perfectionist and desires to put significant amounts of time and energy into one's paid jobs then switching "from work mode to a creative space" is a challenge and, "as a result, poetry usually had to wait for weekends and vacations." Being employed in these fields and continuing to create relies upon maintaining a difficult "work-life balance" and thus "protect[ing] the time [one] needs for creative work."

Alice Major, as mentioned earlier, is also a poet of widely ranging interests, from history to science to the discourse of office workers. Her work in a business-related environment, like Shreve, along with being a journalist, has greatly influenced her choice of subjects and her fascination with "real-world" lexicons. She elaborates:

I don't think I could have written *The Office Tower Tales* if I didn't have the experience of working in office towers myself. It's not just that the working world gives you insight into people who are *not* poets, as well as narrative ideas. It also gives you a whole lot of metaphors that you wouldn't encounter otherwise. Every kind of work has its dialect and dictionary. Also, I have never really wanted to write for other poets – I have always just assumed that the audience is broader than that. So you write about subjects that non-poets might be interested in. So much poetry of the last half-century has become so reflexively writing-about-poetry that it is of minimal interest to people outside our field. The greatest compliments I've had are comments like, "I know those women." (interview)

Major's *Intersecting Sects* discusses the importance of poets working out in the world rather than in academia. "The inability to practice poetry as a paying profession is actually our secret weapon," she asserts, "we are forced out into the world to do the kinds of things that other people do. Chaucer the civil servant, Keats the doctor, Alice the office worker. I don't argue that poets must do exotic things or travel to exotic places to be interesting. But we need a kind of interpenetrability with the larger world to write works that will engage with an audience." She emphasizes, metaphorically connecting poets with other kinds of workers in society: "Poets are like scientists who have to connect their work with experimental success outside the academy, or carpenters who have received their journeyman's tickets and go out to fit cabinets in a real kitchen."

Kate Braid, a Vancouver poet, actually went out and undertook the latter challenge. She recalls: "I got a job as a labourer in construction just to make some quick money but I promptly fell in love with the work. Over the next fifteen years I was a carpenter's helper, apprentice carpenter, journey carpenter (earning a Red Seal ticket) and self-employed contractor. I was active in the Vancouver local of the Carpenters Union and later taught construction apprentices at BCIT [British Columbia Institute of Technology]. During my time in the trade I worked union and non-union, building houses, high-rises, bridges, SkyTrain stations and doing renovations." She believes firmly that her

construction jobs were vital to becoming a writer of both poetry and non-fiction. Because the job was so lonely – for years I didn't even know of other women doing the work, let alone work with any – and the culture so foreign, I resorted to keeping myself company by journal writing. Every night I came home and wrote three to four pages.... As I worked six- and seven-day weeks, nine and ten and twelve hours a day, I was very physically tired and started to shorten my lines, get to the point faster so I could go to bed. I'd always read a lot and loved poetry, and one day realized that was what I was writing.

So the physical challenges of my job made writing a very part-time job but the emotional challenges kept me writing. I later began recording oral histories of working people and teaching students to do the same. I'm forever grateful to Tom Wayman (my first writing teacher) for guiding me in this.

While she resists generalizing the importance of jobs outside of academe for everyone, she also asserts powerfully:

I don't think I'd ever have had the confidence – dared – to write or publish prose, let alone poetry, if construction work had not pushed me. I've written nine books of prose and poetry and numerous essays about various forms of work – fishing, mining, painting and piano playing, in addition to construction. I think work outside teaching literature (which I also did for twelve years) leavens the theoretical aspects of writing. Brings it down to earth in a way that lets it connect to "ordinary" readers. One of the high points in my writing life was when some of us got up the nerve (in about 1984) to put on a performance at the Cultch in Vancouver that was entirely songs and poems about work: secretarial, social work, medicine, construction and more.

She concludes by remembering the audience's excited support, surmising, "if anything showed me how important it is to reflect people's work back at them, to honour it with our literature, that did."

A perhaps equally uncommon vocational path for a writer is Dennis E. Bolen's experience of working many years as a correctional officer. He describes briefly how he started in this line of employment and where it took him: "I'd worked as a community volunteer with BC Corrections so it was a short leap to the federal parole service. I never looked back – ranging over the city and across the country, rampaging as a self-appointed avenging angel, deeming fairness on both sides as I saw fit." Bolen asserts that this job gave him much material for his novels and poems, and he states confidently that all he undertook as a parole officer "has contributed to the Canadian literary scene."

A perhaps more ambivalent response to the effect alternative jobs to academe have had on his writing comes from Ottawa poet and owner of "a small consulting company providing IT services to public utilities for automated design and data integration," Stephen Brockwell. His job, he acknowledges, has brought him a good living and, most importantly, the chance to travel. "I've travelled nearly a million miles for work," Brockwell enthuses, going everywhere from Berne to New Zealand to Japan for his job, an opportunity that can be exhilarating and provide much material for poems, particularly in the chance he has had to "listen to hundreds of voices...and keep notes on what other people say." But it can also be "chaotic, demanding and exhausting." First obtaining a degree in math and computer science, then "working as a statistician in the geocartographics department of Statistics Canada," Brockwell feels that the IT job he now holds just happened for him unwittingly. While he can't recommend this type of work for poets as he thinks "no one should recommend what someone else should do," he does claim that his paid work "intersects with poetry for me in this: the language and structure of a software program has some intersection with the language and structure of a poem," while conceding that he tries "to write poems that subvert the obvious rational path of thinking. Poems are my act of rebellion."

There are other ways to "free range" as a writer. Christine Lowther, a poet who lives in Clayoquot Sound on Vancouver Island, chose deliberately to break free of her full-time job in retail in order to live "half the year off the grid and off-line" in a floathouse. In this space, she has plenty of time to read, work on poems and think. Other benefits are: "quiet, living alone, free rent, lots and lots of time outside, peak experiences, amazement, the unexpected." Of course, in taking any risks to live life differently as a poet, one faces certain challenges. For Lowther, living on a floathouse has also entailed dealing with: "storms, boat problems, leaks, running out of supplies, being cold, being out of touch with publishers and mentors, [and much] loneliness and isolation." However, she feels that breaking out of the comfort zone of living in an expensive but more amenable urban locale has offered her much insight into the risks one must also take to compose powerful poems, while bringing her closer to the natural world that comprises much of her subject matter.

Harold Rhenisch worked for many years cultivating orchards around 100 Mile House, undertaking such tasks as "pruning fruit trees and thinning fruit trees and scything grass." He describes the process of learning language and then poetry beautifully, as forces that grew in him through the act of working in the world.

> I learned poetry from scything grass. You have to do it with your body. You have to dance with the scythe. You have a single point that you draw through the grass, and then the grass is virtually cut by itself, as if with a laser...It's a matter of balance and a perfect line. I learned poetry from pruning fruit trees, often in the half dark or the dark. I learned it by having a childhood that did not include many moments of leisure. Even as a boy, my time was largely spent working with the physical things of the world. I remember thinning apple trees and vanishing completely into the world, and only coming back from the trance four hours later, with the

evidence behind me of a full row of apple trees, thinned by my hands. In the interval, though, I was the air, and the wind, and the mountains, and the trees.

Working in a natural environment, participating in physical labour and learning to honour non-human beings was all a part of finding his way into and through poetry as an organic mode of creation for Rhenisch.

Jenna Butler concurs. The Edmonton poet and teacher recharges her poetic energy by running a small farm in northern Alberta.

Working with my hands makes sense to me, slows the frantic pace of the outside world and gives me time to observe and contemplate. My husband and I run a market garden and live off grid, so most of our time is spent working with whatever the weather throws at us and living an existence predominantly bound by available daylight. I need to be outside under the sky to have a sense of purpose, and the long hours of non-mechanized work on our farm become a form of meditation, a deep and total observation of the everyday. On the Prairies, which can be scant and harsh for much of the year, this observation is attuned to the little things: the smallest shifting of light, the scent of poplar buds breaking. The attention to minute detail appears throughout my poetry and essays.

Garry Gottfriedson, a poet who resides in Kamloops, BC, also believes that having a job and lifestyle that connects the writer to his or her natural environment is essential. Along with other roles,

Gottfriedson spends much of the year ranching. He enthuses, "Working with my horses on my ranch offers an escape that drives my poetic voice and creativity. I call the laborious work I do on my ranch 'thinking with my hands.' It is the time when ideas come to me. Perhaps it happens through a poetic line that rolls across my mind or an image that sends me rushing to the keyboard to open the gates, thus, a poem is born." As these poets show, living and working outside expected realms is not only valuable for their own writing, but for the art of poetry in general. The goal is diversity. In North America we often don't expect poems to emerge from blue-collar workers because we think only the university educated are interested in reading and writing. This belief has shortchanged both artists and their audiences. When writers feel free to hold a range of jobs and pursue a number of different kinds of lifestyles then the literary community will only soar wider and higher.

# A Way of Life: Toward the Impossibility of Summation

*Poetry, for Arthur, might be cleverness, mere icing on the cake; for Orestes it was a life.*
– James Merrill, *The (Diblos) Notebook*

So many words, from myself, fifty-eight Canadian poets, and a host of other American and international writers, to say a few simple, but often forgotten things, about living as an artist in the world. Writing poetry is not about making an income, courting academic prestige or coming out on top on the shaky pyramid of pseudo-fame. Poems, Mary Ruefle says, are "wandering little drift[s] of unidentified sound," which, to me, means mystery, craft, music and, always, ineffability. The practices under discussion and exploration in *The Other 23 & a Half Hours* are both means of grounding poetry within the "houses" of other mediums, of enlarging its perimeters and, in doing so, of drawing it into community engagements that intend to make poetry matter in all the wild and serious ways it can.

What has been happening to poetry in North America over the past century is an increasing lodging in the academy. Complaints against this reality are often viewed as requests for a return to some mythical time in the past where poetry meant something to common people. My position is that an art form constrained by either in-stitutional parameters or calls for absurd supposedly working-class accessibility is weakened. Poetry, as with art in general, thrives on freedom and diversity. A poem is a channel for energy and energy is best created in an environment in which the focus is on the art itself: how it manifests, connects, flourishes and sends out ecstatic and exploratory roots. Confining poetry to one kind of coursing is equivalent to what is done to waterways beneath a city when they are enclosed in cement and forced to follow a singular path.

Let's "daylight" these streams and bring the writing of poems to a place where it can thrive in multiple rivulets, fed by a range of sources. To carry the water metaphor further, instead of relegating ourselves to a homogeneous ecosystem where the pond is sluggish and there are only a few lily pads – publication, teaching jobs, grants and awards – why don't we remember there's a whole ocean out there, none of which our artmaking needs to decline in the aim of becoming as dynamic as possible.

While the subtitle of this book, *Or Everything You Wanted to Know that Your M.F.A. Didn't Teach You,* may have been half tongue in cheek, it is also a shout-out to the system to encourage a deeper emphasis on poetic craft, and particularly on instruction in the palette of forms, on performance skills and on ceasing to insist on a direct line between a writing degree and a teaching job as a *de rigueur* aspect of being a poet in North America.

*The Other 23 & a Half Hours* wants to remind you as a poet that there is time beyond writing the poem, and perhaps thinking of which periodical it would fit in, to interact with the whole community: of poets, of other types of artists, of different kinds of people and life experiences. To recall the quote at the beginning of this conclusion, the poem is not only cleverness, not "mere icing on the cake."

The poem matters first. But the poem, in its singing, can take you into so many practices unimaginable without the poem. You lucky poet you.

# The Appendices
# or Some Things I Have
# Learned (or Overheard)
# Along the Way

Writerly advice usually falls into two types: Rilkean-style *Letters to a Young Poet*, offering a philosophical approach to writing as a kind of spiritual path designed to enlighten one, or the more typical modern type, a book of prompts designed to give the writer fuel for inspiration of the direct-to-page sort with suggestions of how and where to publish once the "product" is finished.

When I have performed in high schools or given workshops at community colleges, the most commonly asked questions have surrounded topics like Making a Living as a Poet, Sending Work to Magazines, Remaining Inspired, Maintaining Discipline and Finding a Publisher. But I don't want to answer any of these burning questions here. *The Other 23 & a Half Hours* has aimed at being neither of these advice types and so it is apropos that the appendices give, instead, practical and sometimes quirky tips, from a range of perspectives, on how to tangibly accomplish what we've been discussing in these pages. So I invite you to listen in as myself and others point you toward memorization techniques, hints on how to run a reading series, ideas on what do to with your book reviews and ways to increase your risk-taking in performing, revision and travel, among other compelling subjects.

# Appendix A:Revisions

The important thing is to not be afraid of revision. Some poems scream for a lot; some appear to be near perfect on arrival. The more you read and revise, the better you will know the difference. Some of my tried-and-tested approaches are:

1. Recite every poem aloud after you've written it, test out each word on your tongue, then put it aside awhile.
2. Writing in longhand versus on a keyboard seems to strengthen the revision process. You can see all the separate drafts more clearly and the reasons why changes were made. The work of editing is undertaken at a deeper somatic or physical level when one is handwriting too.
3. Write the poem out again and see if you would make the same word choices, then recite aloud once or many times more. Ask yourself if each word, image or line break is what the poem truly needs or if you can strengthen it somehow.
4. If you are part of a writers group take it to them and note their opinions, then decide later which ones are valid and usable.

The poem, and your poetic practice in general, can only benefit from such attention.

# Appendix B: Memorization Techniques

When first beginning to memorize, start with a simple poem with a set form and straightforward rhyme scheme. Don't be embarrassed to begin with children's poems such as Dennis Lee's "Alligator Pie" or Shel Silverstein's "One Inch Tall":

If you were only one inch tall, you'd ride a worm to school.
The teardrop of a crying ant would be your swimming pool.
A crumb of cake would be a feast
And last you seven days at least,
A flea would be a frightening beast
If you were one inch tall.

The form is predictable and the rhyme schemes repeat frequently (aabbbc/ddeeec/ffgggc), allowing for easy memorization. And memorizing a children's poem can remind us of the sounds we relished when first learning the language. Additionally, as with the Silverstein example, children's poems are usually full of images (school/pool/door/spider's thread/gum), rather than abstractions. Their vivid qualities make them simpler to recollect.

But regardless of whether you choose children's verse or a work written for adults like Robert Frost's "Mending Wall," the question is how to start to memorize a poem?

The best thing to do is to print out a copy of the poem and carry it with you everywhere. Read it in your head, recite it aloud and try to become as familiar with it as possible, engraining the rhythms into your blood and deeply absorbing the images. If you drive, record it so you can hear yourself reciting it throughout the day.

After this, break the poem down into manageable segments. For some, starting with one line and building to two works. For others, taking it stanza by stanza is more helpful. As Jim Holt notes, memorizing incrementally is an ideal approach. Once you can recite the whole poem, put it aside for a while to let it sink in.

Then return to it. Recite it to others privately. Repeat it to yourself before sleep. If you forget a line or word, glance at the page, then return to the memorized recitation. Before long, the poem will come easily to you and even enter your mind at random moments. Once memorized, it is unlikely that you will ever entirely forget the poem.

The more poems you memorize, the simpler it will become to remember others. Memorizing poetry will increase your facility with form, rhythm, line breaks and other aspects of prosody. And along the way, it will allow you to increase your intimate connection to poetry.

## Some Canadian Poems I'd Recommend Memorizing:

I suppose these poems, many from earlier on in the history of Canadian poetry, have stuck in my mind because they are more formal, resonant or hold levels of personal meaning. Of course, any poem is open to memorization!

Milton Acorn, "Live with Me on Earth under the Invisible Daylight
   Moon"
Earle Birney, "The Bear on the Delhi Road"
Stephanie Bolster, "On the Steps of the Met"
Marilyn Bowering, "St. Augustine's Pear Tree"
Diana Brebner, "I am with You, Breathing the Burning Air"
Bliss Carman, "Low Tide on Grand Pré"
George Elliott Clarke, "King Bee Blues"
Don Coles, "Sometimes All Over"
Sue Goyette, "The New Mothers"
E. Pauline Johnson, "The Song My Paddle Sings"
D. G. Jones, "Death of a Hornet"
Irving Layton, "The Bull Calf"
Pat Lowther, "Riding Past"
Gwendolyn MacEwen, "Dark Pines Under Water"
John Newlove, "Ride Off Any Horizon"
Barbara Nickel, "Three Poems for Violin"
P. K. Page, "T-Bar"
Al Pittman, "April"
E. J. Pratt, "Newfoundland"
Al Purdy, "Say the Names"
John Thompson, "The Change"
Russell Thornton, "The Eyes of Travel"
Anne Wilkinson, "Still Life"

# Appendix C: Incorporating Research and Creative Non-Fiction Techniques into Poems

Poets can benefit tremendously from learning techniques more commonly used by fiction or non-fiction writers. Almost all prose writers draw on research to create their stories or essays and then, particularly in the case of creative non-fiction writers, fuse their reading and analysis with their personal experiences to compose their final narratives. Writing a poem doesn't have to start with an either/or approach; that is, either this poem will be personal or it will be based in research. I find that often when I begin with research, the poem or the book inevitably locates an intimate angle in material that seemed completely foreign to me. Here are several ideas on how you might want to fold research into the composition of your poems:

1. Pick a historical figure that you find compelling. Using the library and Internet, write down as many facts, anecdotes and, especially, key scenes from this individual's life as you can. Organize this material chronologically or according to particular images or themes that you discover. Write some poems based on all this research. Try writing from the perspective of your historical muse, from your own and from the point of view of a central

or even peripheral person in your figure's life. Examine how the poem shifts in tone, rhythm and form when you alter perspective and point of view. Don't be afraid to work with the diction, slang, archaisms and syntax of the era; try developing a unique approach to the character's voices and dramatic situations.

2. Interview people in your own life: family, co-workers, friends. Select a particular focus for your questions that appeals to you – reasons for moving to Canada, perceptions of their work, experiences with men or women – and gather material on this theme. Then write a sequence of poems that explores different facets of this subject matter, perhaps weaving in actual quotes to highlight various aspects of your approach to the topic.

3. Seek out new and unfamiliar environments. Spend time in a hospital waiting room, a morgue, a recycling plant, a retirement home, an automotive shop. Or even just take a bus going downtown on a Friday night. Research here will involve observation, conversations or interviews, reading related to the place and simply just soaking in the sensory details of this foreign and perhaps uncomfortable realm. Meld quotes from texts with direct experiences. Write poems that tell the stories of these places, connecting them to your own narratives or contrasting your perspectives.

4. Write form poems as another kind of research. Look up the rules for structured modes of writing from French villanelles to Vietnamese Lục Bát II poems and add those abilities to your palette as a poet. Even if you only compose one poem in that particular form, the process of integrating a new approach to rhyme or rhythm, line breaks and stanza shape can only expand your skills as a poet and your interest in the history of poetry itself.

Remember: keep your research organized, whether it's on index cards or in folders on your desktop. Seek out as many sources as possible on your subject matter. After researching, let the material sink down within you. Wait. The facts will have a better chance of being transformed into art with patience, concentration and an immersion in the material.

Here is a selective list of some of the poetry books I have read that incorporate research into their poems:

**Books by Canadian poets on Canadian history:**
Margaret Atwood, *The Journals of Susanna Moodie*
George Elliott Clarke, *Execution Poems*
David Day, *The Visions and Revelations of St. Louis the Métis*
Don Gutteridge, *Coppermine: The Quest for North*
Don Gutteridge, *Riel: A Poem for Voices*
John B. Lee, *Godspeed*
Florence McNeil, *Barkerville*
Florence McNeil, *The Overlanders*
Ted Plantos, *Passchendaele*
E. J. Pratt, *The Titanic*
E. J. Pratt, *Towards the Last Spike*
Yvonne Trainer, *Tom Three Persons*

**Books on the lives of artists:**
John Barton, *West of Darkness*
Stephanie Bolster, *Inside A Tent of Skin: 9 Poems from the National Gallery of Ottawa*
Kate Braid, *To This Cedar Fountain*

**Books grounded in nature and ecology:**
Ken Belford, *Ecologue*
Stephanie Bolster, *A Page from the Wonders of Life on Earth*
Di Brandt, *Now You Care*
John Donlan, *The Green Man*
Don McKay, *Strike/Slip*
John Pass, *Water Stair*

# Appendix D: Writing and Placing a Book Review in Canadian Literary Journals

Two different kinds of reviews exist: an overview and a critical approach. Most reviews in Canada tend toward the overview; they describe what the subject matter of the book of poems is, how the text is structured and what forms or styles are used. They exist less to critique the work than to let readers know it exists, to praise it and to promote it for the authors and publishers. A critical approach to the book review, however, must feature a certain amount of analysis, including an evaluation of the quality, meaning and significance of the book within its context. A critical book review is a reaction piece that addresses both the strengths and weaknesses of a collection. Such a review may include a statement of what the author has aimed to do, an evaluation of this attempt and supporting evidence.

Yet there is no one right way to write a book review. Book reviews are highly personal and reflect the hopefully well-considered, educated opinions of the reviewer. A review can be as short as one hundred words or as long as 1,500, depending on the review's purpose and the requirements of the particular journal or website the review has been composed for.

Standard book reviewing procedures may include:

- Information about the title, author, date and copyright

- Informed arguments relating to the work's originality and intent
- An approach to the type of poetry under review, whether of form or school
- A discussion of poetic devices utilized

Read the journals you wish to submit reviews to first, in order to get a sense of their style and approach. Some magazines will accept already written reviews; others will send you the book they want reviewed and give you a deadline for the review's composition. Some even pay! Reviews can be themed or open, concern several authors at once or be in-depth engagements with one text. Query if in doubt.

**Canadian Magazines that Publish Book Reviews:**
*The Antigonish Review*
*ARC Poetry Magazine*
*BC Studies*
*Brick*
*Canadian Literature*
*Canadian Notes and Queries*
*Canadian Poetry*
*Contemporary Verse 2*
*The Dalhousie Review*
*Event*
*The Fiddlehead*
*The Malahat Review*
*Memewar*
*The Nashwaak Review*
*Poetry is Dead*

*Prairie Fire*
*Queen's Quarterly*
*Quill and Quire*
*SubTerrain*
*University of Toronto Quarterly*
*Vallum*

**Canadian Poetry Book Review Blogs:**
Of course, the array of review options is constantly changing but here are a few tried-and-true online sites to look for:
*Canadian Poetries,* http://www.canadianpoetries.com/
*Fresh Raw Cuts,* http://freshrawcuts.blogspot.ca/
*Lemon Hound,* http://lemonhound.blogspot.ca/
*Northern Poetry Review,* http://www.northernpoetryreview.com/
*PoetryReviews.ca,* http://www.poetryreviews.ca/
*Today's Book of Poetry,* http://michaeldennispoet.blogspot.ca/
and my own *Marrow Reviews* at https://crowgirl11.wordpress.com/

# Appendix E: Techniques for Translating Other Poets

1. **Gain an Intimacy with the Poem.** Read the poem again and again until the words become thoroughly familiar to your tongue. In such a way, you will be able to feel the rhythm of the poem: its pace, breath pauses, cadences and nodes of energy. Write the poem in longhand and make ten copies. Post these up around your house or office. This process will increase your knowledge of the poem's grammatical structure: where the verbs are, where there is a shift in tenses, how the line breaks function.

2. **Become Familiar with the Poet.** If you are lucky enough to pick a living poet to translate, get to know them so you can ask him or her questions about the poem. Why did they select this form? What does this or that word connote? Why did they include this particular image? The more you know about the poet's poem, the better able you are to comprehend the work's nuances from within. If you have selected a dead poet or an inaccessible one, there will be additional challenges. Find out as much as you can about the poet's life through research.

3. **Stick as Close as You can to the Original Poem.** When you translate a poem, you should try to attend to the meaning and intent of the poem as much as possible. That said, you also have artistic license to attempt to render a lucid and graceful

translation. Enjoyment of the poem's sounds and form is paramount, not just the message of the piece. Some words, especially slang, idiom or neologisms, are impossible to translate. It is thus important in such a case to be creative in locating an approximate term that provides the closest possible sense the poet intended.

4.  **Do the Work Yourself.** Although there are wonderful dictionaries and online guides to assist with translation, you should only use these computer programs and dictionary translations as models. They may help you to access the basic structure of the poem but your aim is to place live language on this skeletal frame and make the poem breathe again in its new language.

5.  **Prepare for Multiple Drafts and be Patient.** When you finish a translation, put it aside for several weeks. Then take time to think about something else, in your own language. At this point, return to the poem and see what's missing and what's working. Translating a poem is a lot like writing a poem. It takes time, energy, thought and ability. Inviting poems into another language is one of the most beautiful means through which we can share cultures, honour other poets and poetry itself, and remind ourselves that we can transcend the limitations of geography and time.

# Appendix F: How to Host a
# Radio Show

As I have not run a radio show myself, here are a few pointers from two seasoned hosts.

## Bruce Kauffman:

1. Music: It should factor – just a couple of songs in the hour – one midway through and another at the end to slide out on. I do promote local musicians whenever I can find recordings – but attempt to tie the music to the preceding poet and bleed right into the song without that silent break between. Personally, I don't download songs – I have my own stash and the station has an extensive library.

2. Editing: As for the readings/events themselves – I burn everything to disc, because I'm comfortable with using that in the studio when I'm on air. I edit readings only for sound quality and to cut prolonged pieces of dead air/unnecessary monologue – I do not edit for content. Editing is done in studio with a program called Sound System, which graphically, in a band, displays that which has been recorded and then enters into it. It's a tool allowing a person to select any portion of the recording to cut, amplify, de-amplify and break into segments, which, then on the CD, become the tracks. This editing process usually

takes about two hours, depending on both the length of the reading and on the diversity of voices and the number of people reading.

3.  Recording: The show itself should always be live – never pre-recorded. Any poet/author whose work is appearing on the show must be notified at least a few days in advance of the show and (in all applicable places) allowed to grant permission first. Prepare the show – research the guest's life/work for live interviews/readings. For shows without a guest – spend time selecting and sequencing poets and music, complete a run-sheet with timelines and research to include announcements of local and semi-local events.

4.  Promotion and Preparation: Promote the show weekly and religiously, and eventually others will offer to help promote the show as well. I believe that, including promotion, I spend roughly four to six hours each week to develop a one-hour show, and in the summer months and winter break probably six to eight hours for the expanded two-hour show. Partly for promotion's sake and partly for that of consistency, I'm always working on the show two to three weeks ahead – having already solidly tied up the shows for the coming two weeks.

S. R. Duncan:

The best advice I would give anyone looking to produce any regular show, be it radio, television or a live event, is to find someone with complementary skills to partner up with on- and/or off-air.

Believe it or not, a half-hour show can be a lot of commitment. It's not just the on-air time, which requires physically being at the station to operate the control board (remote broadcasts used to be difficult to coordinate and pre-recording would still require someone at the studio to play the show for broadcast), but there is all the off-air administration involved too: that is, booking guests, archiving shows, updating a website and posting to Facebook or other social networking sites. Then there is also the live fundraising and audience-building events, which also require effort and coordination. So join forces!

# Appendix G: Running a Poetry Reading Series

Let's start with my hints for how best to run a series and then hear from Joe Blades, also a long-term promoter!

## How to Begin:

First decide what kind of reading you want to host. There are events that only feature published writers and not other kinds of arts, performances that have open mics or poetry slams and series that also offer musicians as part of the bill. Some series are formal and others are casual. Some take place every week while others happen every month. If you choose the type that suits your schedule and varied tastes then it will likely work best in the long run.

## Picking a Venue:

It's important in choosing a place to run a reading series that one "finds an owner who really wants to have a reading in their place – not just to build traffic," according to long-time host Larry Jaffe. The venue can be a café, a bar, a library, a college or university. The event can even take place in your home. Ask whether there's a sound system. Check if the owner will provide a bar tab to invited guests. See if the host is responsible for cleanup. Think about whether silence is essential or if it's not so important if the latte machine starts up or a stranger walks in off the street. If you feel comfortable with the chosen venue, the guests will too.

## Getting the Performers:

Start with friends and acquaintances who are local artists. Ask them to perform. The word will get out and soon people will be eager to read at your series. Apply to the Canada Council or the League of Canadian Poets for more well-known authors or those who aren't in the immediate neighbourhood. The Writers' Union of Canada is another option. Be aware that these organizations charge series hosts a small administrative fee.

Once word spreads about your series, publishers will contact you to set up events for authors on tour. Open mics are another way to find performers. Let ten people sign up per event. Give them three minutes each. Pick the best of them to be feature readers at a later date.

## Promoting the Event:

Place free ads in local newspapers. For a small fee, the university radio station will play your ad for up to two weeks prior to the event. Create a poster for each reading, including a brief bio of the author, and post it up around the area at least a week beforehand.

Establish an email list through a sign-up sheet available at each event. Use Twitter and Facebook or other social networking sites to promote the series. Ask for RSVPs to better plan the set-up of the room and the amount of refreshments if any.

## Being a host:

Be prepared. Obtain short bios from the performers at least a week in advance. Make sure they are up-to-date ones and then practice reading them. This way mistakes and a feeling of discomfort will be lessened. Ask the performers when they arrive what arrangements suit them. Standing or sitting? A lectern or a chair? The most apropos reading order based on whether you have local or travelling, seasoned or up-and-coming poets? Provide water. Let them know what the refreshments are, if there's a bar tab, where the washroom is.

Organize the event so there's a break in the middle. The audience likes to stretch, get drinks or buy books. Set up a book table and get someone to run it efficiently. Pay the guests, either through grants from the funding bodies or through donations at the door. Be friendly and respectful. Thank the performers sincerely at the end of the night. In this manner, both writers and the audience will remember this enjoyable series.

## A few additional suggestions for potential reading series hosts from Joe Blades:

1. Decide upfront what the mission or mandate of your reading series will be. Whether it's an open mic series, a featured writer and open mic, multiple featured writers on the same bill, a writer plus a musician on the same bill or other formats. Poets, fiction writers, novelists, playwrights and/or spoken word/performance poets?

2. Choose a venue carefully: are there rental fees, meal and drink minimums, is it licensed or not, can you collect admission or donations, is there a sound system, is it accessible, kid-friendly, what day of the week, time of day, parking, quietness, private room, televisions over the bar, non-reading patrons, promotion requirements/tie-ins, reader/performer fees or no fees, Canada Council or other funded readers or not? All this needs to be considered.

3.  Get ready to deal with schedule wrangling many months in advance, especially for funded readings and author promotion tours for new books. We live in Canada so be prepared for bad weather, especially winter storms. I've had readers arrive just before or in snowstorms that make the reading or reading tour impossible to do, or the readers don't/can't arrive on time (and then you have to deal with the tour funders/backers).

4.  Sometimes you encounter problematic author egos and high expectations. Not always the case, but it definitely happens. Be prepared to field questions and deal with inflated hopes for publicity, audience or remuneration.

5.  The Canada Council for the Arts per reading travel allowance is usually inadequate for a single reading so tours to multiple venues and hosts is encouraged or required. They also do not cover writer accommodation or meals en route or in the community and they expect hosts to cover those services or expenses. The Canada Council for the Arts does allow reading hosts to charge a reasonable admission to events, as a means of host fundraising, or the host has to raise funds elsewhere, find other sponsors or foot the bill personally. The Writers' Union of Canada (TWUC) and the League of Canadian Poets (LCP) reading programs charge host administration fees (TWUC, $75/full reading and LCP $50/full reading) for readings approved for funding through those organizations, and they have a lower travel allowance than the Canada Council for the Arts. Again, the host has to make other arrangements for funding, has to have dollars themselves to pay the difference or the writer/author/reader has to have means to make the tour happen.

6. Hosting a reading series can be very rewarding, but it is easy to take on too much. Try not to go overboard or you will burn out. Like a marathoner, you have to pace yourself. Furthermore, just because you host a reading series, you do not have to say yes to every writer/author who asks you for a reading. No matter where you are, there likely are other potential reading series hosts. You can share the organizing, pass the baton and/or host multiple reading series. Enjoy!

# Appendix H: How to Start an Online Zine and How to Make and Sell Old-Fashioned Chapbooks

Mark McCawley advises:
Publishing online depends largely upon what you want to do, and what you want to publish. There are quite a few web publishing platforms, the two most popular (and free) being Blogger, a weblog publishing tool from Google, for sharing text, photos and video; and WordPress, a personal publishing platform with a focus on aesthetics, web standards and usability.

Blogger is an excellent tool for publishing general information, events coverage, press releases, interviews, reviews, the occasional poem, short story and novel excerpts. It even functions well for promoting and publishing tour itinerary and video excerpts from tour readings.

As for starting an online magazine, I would recommend WordPress. The platform has two tiers – a wordpress.com tier that is free of charge (with limited functionality), and a wordpress.org tier that one does pay for, which has various levels and modes of functionality. I have begun my own online magazine using this free wordpress.com tier, while determining the magazine's long-term requirements of space and storage before accessing the next tier and paying for a domain name.

At this stage, the functionality and interactivity of the magazine will also increase more substantially than with the first tier. Also, be prepared for an ever-increasing learning curve, as with more functionality and interactivity one sees a rise in daily editorial responsibility too.

In terms of how to put chapbooks, pamphlets and broadsides together – you can go from the pretty basic cut-and-paste technique to the highly technical desktop publishing approach using Microsoft Word, QuarkXPress, Adobe PageMaker and InDesign. Both approaches are worthwhile and valuable.

It is not the publishing standards that you have that solely determine whether or not your publication will be a good one, it is what you do with those publishing standards that you have at hand.

Running a small press is a labour of love but there are ways to both make it cost-effective and to distribute its materials appropriately from zine and small press fairs as utilized frequently by small presses like rob mclennan's Chaudiere Books to mail order lists as with David Zieroth's Alfred Gustav Press.

Jenna Butler is one such small press publisher. Here she explains her unique approach:

Since 2004, I've worked on chapbook design with other poets and artists through Rubicon Press.

The chapbooks we design are made to be laser printed and saddle-stitched; they need to be simply and sturdily crafted so that they ship well and are relatively inexpensive for buyers. The press's mandate is to publish excellent poets from around the world and to make their work available to all at a reasonable cost.

We've had many fortunate pairings with artists and photographers who have donated cover art, and the use of fly-leaves allows us to include a variety of textured papers in the books.

It's important to develop loyal connections with collaborators. For instance, we've worked with a print shop in Edmonton since 2004 and have developed a great relationship – they now know the ins and outs of chapbook printing very well and can fill an order on really short notice. Plus it's neat to know that their handiwork is being posted off to the US, India, England and elsewhere.

There are lots of places where you can find information on how to make and bind chapbooks. The Poets & Writers website (http://www.pw.org/content/diy_how_to_make_and_bind_chapbooks?cmnt_all=1) has a particularly good selection of videos and diagrams and is a helpful place to get started.

# Appendix I: Tips on Making Multimedia Creations

Videopoems are not just short films, but visual representations of poetry. Usually the poet will recite the poem and the filmmaker (who may also be the poet) will shoot imagery to accompany the piece that may echo the words, interpret them or take an entirely divergent direction that makes, in essence, its own work of art. Music and text can also be included. The Poets & Writers website (http://www.pw.org/content/six_video_poems), to give one example, has collected several wonderful selections from the medium, which show the range of possibilities open to videopoem creators. And here are two videopoem makers to offer their perspectives on working in this particular form of multimedia:

## Kath MacLean:

Making videopoems is a learning experience. It's a different genre and that keeps me interested. Funding however is very limited. If you are with a university and they offer some sort of creative scholarship, go for it. Most of my funding came this way. Be ready to pay for much of it yourself. Do it in steps – baby steps. 1) Write the poem. 2) See if it has enough story and narrative to float. 3) Test the images for story potential. 4) Have a vision in your head before you approach your team. 5) Figure out a budget based on what you currently have. 6) Keep hoping you will get a grant. It is really hard. Some do, many don't. Write to your budget. 7) Don't give up. Keep at it and recognize it takes longer than you want it to. Realize it might not happen *now*. Don't be embarrassed if you didn't get any money or feel no one cares. You have to keep moving on the basis of your own steam. If your videopoem matters enough to you, it will eventually get made.

## Heather Haley:

I work with digital video because it is accessible and affordable, important considerations for most poets. A high-definition camera can now be acquired for approximately five hundred dollars. I don't have to settle for a lower quality image either. Using the poem as script, I start with a shot list and storyboard. I see it as an adaptation process, adapting voice and text to video. Preparation is crucial. Choose your crew wisely. Get everything in writing. I pay artists half their fee up front and the remainder when the work is completed. Invariably videopoems are produced despite low budgets; one must be inventive and resourceful.

With so many modes of possible creation out there, how do we know what will work for us as writers? Try a few and see!

1. Take a different class at the local community centre every season, experimenting with a range of materials until you find

your additional artistic strengths, then work on combining them with your poems.

2. Go to cafés and bars where they have open stage jams. Bring an instrument and join in. This is not only the way to become more confident and comfortable playing live, but also to meet other musicians who are interested in creating with you.

3. Rent an affordable studio space and set up an easel, a potter's wheel, a sewing machine or other equipment through which to experience free play with other art forms. Don't concern yourself with the outcome; merely enjoy the process.

4. Select a poem or a sequence of pieces and imagine how you would turn your poetry into a painting, a song, a dance piece or a sculpture. Take photographs and write poems based on them.

5. Learn how to use a still or video camera and take long walks or bus trips where the intent is to accumulate material and to increase experience.

6. Read the biographies of other kinds of artists for inspiration. Spend time in galleries, go to concerts. Write ekphrastic poems about art or jazz/chorale forms that overtly fuse words and music. Play with words on the page so their concrete forms mirror the movements of dance.

# Appendix J: Collaborative Ideas

Although it is not easy to find a collaborator, starting with online experiments as Stuart Ross or Gregory Betts have done is a good idea, before branching out to "real world" creations with friends or acquaintances as Joe Rosenblatt and I have accomplished. One has to be willing to take risks regardless of the fact that egos are on the line. If a collaboration fails to achieve its potential, try another approach. Always remain discerningly open.

1.  Choose a poetic form open to collaboration like a renga or an epic in heroic couplets and write it with a group, either at a gathering or in an online forum.
2.  Write a glosa that draws four lines from another poet's poem and ends each one of the stanzas with that line. See P. K. Page's book *Hologram* for examples.
3.  Use email or Facebook to write an exquisite corpse or surrealist collage poem with poets across Canada.
4.  Go to open jams and find musicians willing to serve as a backing band for your poems.
5.  Co-write and perform a sound poem with another poet or group.
6.  Work with a dancer to choreograph a poem to their movements and musical selection.

# Appendix K: My Travel Tips
## for Poets

1. Travel alone. It may be less safe but it's also much more likely to produce poetry. With precautions and sense, solo travel won't be dangerous but it will be highly productive. When you travel alone you don't have to worry about a companion's agenda, emotions or well-being. Instead, you can focus on research for the particular project, linger at ruins or museums that might be uninteresting to others or spend hours on writing without guilt.

2. Travel randomly. If you travel on a cruise line or as part of a tour group, you are less likely to work on poems based on the experience. First, your time is more highly controlled; second, your excursions are quite rigidly planned and third, the other participants are likely to prove distracting. Again, as with travelling solo, the risk increases, but so do the potential rewards. Plan your own itinerary but leave plenty of room open for the mysterious and unexpected.

3. Travel to out-of-the-way places. If you want to see Mexico, for instance, don't go to Puerto Vallarta or Cancún. Head to Morelia or Chetumal or dozens of other smaller, less touristy locales where you are likely to have to speak their language, try strange food, stay in less swanky accommodations and otherwise participate in a more enriching time for your art. Or, if your aim is

to compose political poetry, like Gary Geddes, you need to take even more risks and explore continents like Africa for lengthy periods of time in order to become familiarized with some of the issues facing the particular region and to give yourself the chance to steep your senses in this environment.

4. Travel with a notebook. Even though your sense of self may be too disoriented during the trip to work on composing poems, it's always possible to write notes, drafts, ideas and other material that can later be incorporated into pieces when one is home. Transpose fragments of speech, dialect, idiom, place names and words for food or other essential details. When you return home, such a notebook will serve as a guide for the composition of poems, along with your memory and some text-based research.

5. Travel smart. This means that wherever you are planning to travel, read up on the place first. Learn some of its language and know its poets and writers. Not only will your increased knowledge demonstrate a level of respect toward where you are travelling, but it will offer another experiential layer to add to your own direct experiences. The books you read about the locale will then fuse with your particular engagement with the place to produce a unique perception of the journey.

# List of Personal Interviews

Barbour, Douglas. Email to the author, January 6, 2012.

Beach, Kimmy. Email to the author, June 1, 2011.

Betts, Gregory. Email to the author, January 19, 2012.

Blades, Joe. Email to the author, December 31, 2011.

Blomer, Yvonne. Email to the author, June 4, 2014.

Bolen, Dennis E. Email to the author, November 14, 2014.

Braid, Kate. Email to the author, May 29, 2014.

Brockwell, Stephen. Email to the author, July 7, 2014.

Butler, Jenna. Email to the author, March 21, 2015.

Charach, Ron. Email to the author, May 27, 2014.

Dickinson, Adam. Emails to the author, May 28, 2014, and November 12, 2014.

Duncan, S. R. Email to the author, January 13, 2012.

Eddy, Trisia. Email to the author, September 6, 2011.

Edwards, Jannie. Email to the author, February 13, 2012.

Geddes, Gary. Email to the author, January 10, 2012.

Gilpin, Chris. Email to the author, August 20, 2014.

Glickman, Susan. Email to the author, August 29, 2011.

Gottfriedson, Garry. Email to the author, February 13, 2012.

Graham, Catherine. Email to the author, November 14, 2014.

Haley, Heather. Email to the author, September 13, 2011.

Hausner, Beatriz. Email to the author, June 4, 2014.

Heighton, Steven. Email to the author, November 11, 2011.

Hunt, Barbara. Email to the author, February 28, 2011.

Jernigan, Amanda. Email to the author, June 3, 2014.

Kauffman, Bruce. Email to the author, November 25, 2011.

Kishkan, Theresa. Email to the author, November 6, 2014.

Lane, M. Travis. Email to the author, March 18, 2012.

Leclerc, Christine. Email to the author, January 12, 2012.

Leedahl, Taylor. Email to the author, January 11, 2012.

Lemay, Shawna. Email to the author, July 5, 2014.

Lowther, Christine. Email to the author, August 26, 2011.

Mackie, Jeffrey. Email to the author, July 15, 2014.

MacLean, Kath. Email to the author, July 8, 2011.

Major, Alice. Emails to the author, January 23, 2012, and November 14, 2014.

McCaslin, Susan. Emails to the author, February 19, 2012, and May 2, 2013.

McCawley, Mark. Email to the author, November 30, 2011.

mclennan, rob. Email to the author, November 9, 2014.

Mellor, Jane. Email to the author, May 13, 2013.

Meyer, Bruce. Email to the author, August 17, 2013.

Morse, Garry Thomas. Email to the author, January 5, 2012.

Morton, Wendy. Email to the author, June 14, 2014.

Nish, Bonnie. Email to the author, November 9, 2014.

Noyes, Steve. Email to the author, October 16, 2011.

Pass, John. Email to the author, November 8, 2014.

Pilarski, Patrick M. Email to the author, January 23, 2012.

Priest, Robert. Emails to the author, March 23, 2013, and April 7, 2014.

Rawlings, Angela. Email to the author, June 1, 2011.

Rhenisch, Harold. Email to the author, September 19, 2011.

Rosenblatt, Joe. Email to the author, November 15, 2012.

Ross, Stuart. Emails to the author, September 3, 2012, and January 12, 2014.

Rowley, Mari-Lou. Email to the author, September 15, 2011.

Ruzesky, Jay. Email to the author, August 26, 2011.

Shreve, Sandy. Email to the author, June 13, 2014.

Sorestad, Glen. Email to the author, February 2, 2012.

Vermeersch, Paul. Email to the author, January 27, 2015.

Young, Patricia. Email to the author, April 26, 2012.

# Bibliography

Bankston III, Carl L. "Adrift or Foundering?: Students are adrift because college was never intended for mass production of degrees." The John William Pope Center for Higher Education Policy, March 7, 2011. http://www.popecenter.org/commentaries /article.html?id=2487.

Barbour, Douglas, and Sheila E. Murphy. *Continuations*. Edmonton: University of Alberta Press, 2006.

Barwin, Gary. "Listening to Your Own Hive Mind." Interview by Sandra Ridley. *ARC Poetry Magazine* 74 (Summer 2014): 64.

Bernstein, Charles. *My Way: Speeches and Poems*. Chicago: University of Chicago Press, 1999.

Best Colleges Online. "In Praise of Memorization: 10 Proven Brain Benefits." July 23, 2012. http://www.bestcollegesonline.com /blog/2012/07/23/in-praise-of-memorization-10-proven-brain -benefits/.

Betts, Gregory. "The Rise of the Small Press Movement in Canada." Historical Perspectives on Canadian Publishing. http://hpcanpub .mcmaster.ca/case-study/rise-small-press-movement-canada.

Bishop, Elizabeth. *One Art: Letters*. Edited by Robert Giroux. New York: Farrar, Straus and Giroux, 1995.

Bowering, George. *Left Hook: A Sideways Look at Canadian Writing*. Vancouver: Raincoast Books, 2005.

Breaugh, Cate. "Canoeing Poets will Portage in Paris for Special Reading." *Paris Star*, August 5, 2010. http://www.parisstaronline.com/2010/08/05/canoeing-poets-will-portage-in-paris-for-special-reading.

Bukowski, Charles. Quoted in "Charles Bukowski on the Public Perception of Art." NateJordan.com, March 11, 2013. http://natejordan.com/post/45112664126/charles-bukowski-on-the-public-perception-of-art.

Carruth, Hayden. *Selected Essays & Reviews*. Port Townsend, WA: Copper Canyon Press, 1996.

Clay, Steven, and Rodney Phillips. *A Secret Location on the Lower East Side: Adventures in Writing, 1960–1980*. New York: Granary Books, 1998.

Coach House Books. "About Us." Coach House Books. http://www.chbooks.com/about_us.

Cohen, Leonard. "Songwriter Leonard Cohen Discusses Fame, Poetry and Getting Older." Interview by Jeffrey Brown. *PBS NewsHour*, June 28, 2006. http://www.pbs.org/newshour/bb/entertainment-jan-june06-cohen_06-28/.

Collins, Billy. "Words, Words, Words: The Craft of Writing." *Big Think* video, 3:06. July 4, 2007. http://bigthink.com/videos/words-words-words-the-craft-of-writing.

Collis, Stephen. "Phyllis Webb at 85." *Jacket 2*, June 18, 2012. http://jacket2.org/commentary/phyllis-webb-85.

Compton, Wayde. *After Canaan: Essays on Race, Writing, and Region*. Vancouver, BC: Arsenal Pulp Press, 2010.

Corman, Cid. "Poetry for Radio." Communication. *Poetry* 81, no.3 (December 1952).

Creeley, Robert, and Steve Swallow. "Robert Creeley & Steve Swallow: Poetic Collaborations." Poets.org, 2014. http://www.poets.org/poetsorg/text/robert-creeley-steve-swallow-poetic-collaborations.

"David Antin." Poetry Foundation. http://www.poetryfoundation.org/bio/david-antin.

Deresiewicz, William. "The Death of the Artist – and the Birth of the Creative Entrepreneur." *The Atlantic*, December 28, 2014. http://www.theatlantic.com/magazine/archive/2015/01/the-death-of-the-artist-and-the-birth-of-the-creative-entrepreneur/383497/.

Di Prima, Diane. *Recollections of My Life as a Woman: The New York Years*. New York: Penguin Books, 2001.

Disch, Thomas M. *The Castle of Indolence: On Poetry, Poets, and Poetasters*. New York: Picador, 1995.

Dove, Rita. "Brushed by an Angel's Wings." Interview by Grace Cavalieri. In *Conversations with Rita Dove*, edited by Earl G. Ingersoll. Jackson: University Press of Mississippi, 2003. Previously published as "Brushed by an Angel's Wings," *American Poetry Review*, April 1995.

———. "Poet at the Dance: Rita Dove in Conversation." Interview by Robert McDowell. Poets.org, 2003. http://www.poets.org/poetsorg/text/poet-dance-rita-dove-conversation.

Drake, William. *Sara Teasdale: Woman & Poet*. Knoxville: University of Tennessee Press, 1989.

Duhamel, Denise, and Maureen Seaton. "Poetry and Collaboration: Denise Duhamel & Maureen Seaton." Poets.org, 2006. http://www.poets.org/poetsorg/text/poetry-and-collaboration-denise-duhamel-maureen-seaton.

Enszer, Julie R. "Poetry in Translation: A Conversation with Kätlin Kaldmaa." *Huffington Post*, November 6, 2014. http://www .huffingtonpost.com/julie-r-enszer/poetry-in-translation-a -conversation-with-katlin-kaldmaa_b_6097122.html.

Fitzgerald, Judith. "Contemplating Pickton." Review of *Living Under Plastic*, by Evelyn Lau. *Globe and Mail*, August 24, 2010. http://www.theglobeandmail.com/arts/books-and-media /review-living-under-plastic-by-evelyn-lau/article1388860/.

Fitzgerald, Robert. "Robert Fitzgerald." Interview by Edwin Honig. In *The Poet's Other Voice: Conversations on Literary Translation*. Amherst: University of Massachusetts Press, 1985.

Frost, Robert. Introduction to *King Jasper*, by Edwin Arlington Robinson. New York: Macmillan Company, 1935.

Frye, Northrop. "From 'Letters in Canada' 1952." *Northrop Frye – The Bush Garden*, February 2009. http://northropfrye-thebushgarden .blogspot.ca/2009/02/from-letters-in-canada-1952.html. First published 1952 as "Letter in Canada" by *University of Toronto Quarterly*.

———. "From 'Letters in Canada' 1958." *Northrop Frye – The Bush Garden*, February 2009. http://northropfrye-thebushgarden .blogspot.ca/2009/02/from-letters-in-canada-1958.html. First published 1958 as "Letter in Canada" by *University of Toronto Quarterly*.

Ginsberg, Allen. "Audio Interview with Allen Ginsberg." Interview by Don Swaim, February 4, 1985. Wired for Books. http:// www.wiredforbooks.org/Allenginsberg/.

———. Quoted in Jacqueline Gens, "Mind Writing Slogans of Allen Ginsberg," *Poetry Mind*. http://tsetso.blogspot.ca/p/allen -ginsbergs-mind-writing-slogans.html.

Gioia, Dana. "The Arts – Agents of Change and Source of Enchantment: Dana and Ted Gioia discuss literature, music, education, business, culture, and the Catholic Faith." Interview by Carl E. Olson. *Catholic World Report*, October 15, 2013. http://www.catholicworldreport.com/Item/2643/the_artsagents_of_change_and_source_of_enchantment.aspx.

———. "Dana Gioia on the Close Connection between Business and Poetry." Interview by Michael Useem. *Knowledge@Wharton* (May 30, 2007). http://knowledge.wharton.upenn.edu/article/dana-gioia-on-the-close-connection-between-business-and-poetry/.

Hacker, Marilyn. Interview by KC Orcutt. *Barzakh* 3 (Fall 2010–Spring 2011). http://barzakh.net/site/issue-03/2108.

Halfe, Louise. *Bear Bones & Feathers*. Regina, SK: Coteau Books, 1994.

Hall, Donald. *Unpacking the Boxes: A Memoir of a Life in Poetry*. New York: Mariner Books, 2009.

———. *The Weather for Poetry: Essays, Reviews, and Notes on Poetry, 1977–81*. Ann Arbor: The University of Michigan Press, 1982.

Hammond, Raymond P. *Poetic Amusement*. Garden City, NY: Athanata Arts, 2010.

Harbach, Chad. "MFA vs. NYC." *n+1* 10 (Fall 2010). https://nplusonemag.com/issue-10/the-intellectual-situation/mfa-vs-nyc/.

Hayward, Michael. "Unspeakable Visions: The Beat Generation and the Bohemian Dialectic." Essay for CMNS 850: History of Publishing, Simon Fraser University, August 1991. http://www.sfu.ca/~hayward/UnspeakableVisions/page1.html.

Heighton, Steven. *Workbook: Memos & Dispatches on Writing*. Toronto: ECW Press, 2011.

Hemingway, Ernest. "Ernest Hemingway, The Art of Fiction No. 21." Interview by George Plimpton. *The Paris Review* 18 (Spring 1958). http://www.theparisreview.org/interviews/4825/the-art-of-fiction-no-21-ernest-hemingway.

Holt, Jim. "Got Poetry?" *New York Times*, April 2, 2009. http://www.nytimes.com/2009/04/05/books/review/Holt-t.html?_r=0.

Hudgens, Ross. "Why Creativity Requires 'Travel.'" Ross Hudgens, Content Marketing. June 1, 2010. http://www.rosshudgens.com/how-to-be-creative/.

Jaffe, Larry. "The Poetry Kit Interviews Larry Jaffe." The Poetry Kit, 1999. http://www.poetrykit.org/iv/jaffe.htm.

Jamison, Leslie. "Which Creates Better Writers: An MFA Program or New York City?: 'MFA vs NYC' investigates the relationship between creativity and collectivity." *The New Republic*, February 27, 2014. http://www.newrepublic.com/article/116778/mfa-vs-nyc-most-useful-explanation-how-writers-get-paid.

Jones, D. G. "Grounds for Translation." In *The Insecurity of Art: Essays on Poetics*, edited by Ken Norris and Peter Van Toorn. Montreal: Vehicule Press, 1982.

Kay, Barbara. "Wasted Tax Dollars on a Values-Void Novel." *National Post*, January 21, 2015. http://news.nationalpost.com/full-comment/barbara-kay-wasted-tax-dollars-on-a-values-void-novel.

Kessler, Stephen. *Moving Targets: On Poets, Poetry & Translation*. Berkeley, CA: El León Literary Arts, 2008.

Kienapple, Bronwyn. "New Literary Journal Gets Meta with Review on Reviewing." *Torontoist*, September 19, 2011. http://

torontoist.com/2011/09/new-literary-journal-gets-meta-with
-a-review-on-reviewing/.

Koch, Kenneth. *Making Your Own Days: The Pleasures of Reading and Writing Poetry.* New York: Simon & Schuster, 1999.

Kogawa, Joy. *A Choice of Dreams.* Toronto: McClelland & Stewart, 1974.

Konyves, Tom. "Concrete, Visual, Videopoetry: A Model for Teaching Creative *Visual* Writing." Paper presented at the Canadian Creative Writers and Writing Programs Conference, Banff, AB, October 2010. http://www.academia.edu/1479649/Concrete _Visual_Videopoetry_A_Model_for_Teaching_Creative _Visual_Writing.

Kunitz, Stanley. "Stanley Kunitz, The Art of Poetry No. 29." Interview by Chris Busa. *The Paris Review* 83 (Spring 1982). http:// www.theparisreview.org/interviews/3185/the-art-of-poetry -no-29-stanley-kunitz.

Lehrer, Jonah. "Why We Travel." The Observer, *The Guardian,* March 14, 2010. http://www.theguardian.com/travel/2010 /mar/14/why-travel-makes-you-smarter.

Leithauser, Brad. "Why We Should Memorize." *The New Yorker,* January 25, 2013. http://www.newyorker.com/books/page -turner/why-we-should-memorize.

Levi, Peter. *Tennyson.* London: Macmillan, 1993.

Library of Congress staff. "Poet of the Nation." *Revising Himself: Walt Whitman and* Leaves of Grass. Washington, DC: Library of Congress. Last modified August 16, 2010. Exhibition website. http:// www.loc.gov/exhibits/treasures/whitman-poetofthenation .html.

Lista, Michael. "Michael Lista, On Poetry: Publish Less." *National Post*, February 7, 2014. http://news.nationalpost.com/arts/books /michael-lista-on-poetry-publish-less.

Luke, Pearl. "Canadian and US Creative Writing Degree Programs." *Be a Better Writer.* http://www.be-a-better-writer.com/creative -writing-degree.html.

Major, Alice. *Intersecting Sets: A Poet Looks at Science.* Edmonton: University of Alberta Press, 2011.

Medley, Mark. "Found in Translation." *National Post*, February 15, 2013. http://news.nationalpost.com/arts/books/found-in-translation.

Menard, Louis. "Show or Tell: Should creative writing be taught?" *The New Yorker*, June 8, 2009. http://www.newyorker.com /magazine/2009/06/08/show-or-tell.

Merwin, W. S. *The Shadow of Sirius.* Port Townsend, WA: Copper Canyon Press, 2009.

———. "Translator's Notes: Little Soul." *Poetry* (April 2006). http:// www.poetryfoundation.org/poemcomment/177889.

Mewshaw, Michael. "Travel, travel writing, and the literature of travel." Plenary address at the 2004 South Central MLA conference, New Orleans, LA, October 28, 2004. Reproduced at Rolf Potts' Vagabonding, February 22, 2006. http://www.vagablogging .net/michael-mewshaw-on-the-importance-of-travel-to -literature.html.

Miller, Jeremy. "Helen Vendler, Robinson Jeffers, and the transient sickness of *ad hominem* criticism." *Feeding the Bloat*, February 2, 2009. https://thebloath.wordpress.com/2009/02/02/helen-vendler -robinson-jeffers-and-the-transient-sickness-of-ad-hominem -criticism/.

Moore, Marianne. *The Complete Poems of Marianne Moore*. London: Macmillan, 1967.

Morrison, Blake. "Blake Morrison on Anthony Burgess the critic – 'he aspired to know everything.'" *The Guardian*, February 21, 2015. http://www.theguardian.com/books/2015/feb/21/anthony -burgess-book-critic.

Murphy, Sheila E. "Collaborating with Doug Barbour." *Jacket 39* (2010). http://jacketmagazine.com/39/barbour-sheila-murphy .shtml.

Nichol, bp. "The Prose Tattoo: Selected Performance Scores of the Four Horsemen." January 1983. Light & Dust Anthology of Poetry. http://www.thing.net/~grist/l&d/bpnichol/4hm-int.htm.

Norman, Peter. "Red Pen of Fury!" On Writing #39. *Ottawa Poetry Newsletter*, September 12, 2014. http://ottawapoetry.blogspot .ca/2014/09/on-writing-39-peter-norman.html.

Ntuli, Pitika. "Ntuli comes to Museum Africa." City of Johannesburg, March 26, 2010. http://www.joburg.org.za/index .php?option=com_content&task=view&id=5006&Itemid=240.

Orr, David. "From Dissections to Depositions, Poets' Second Jobs." *NPR Books*, April 29, 2013. http://www.npr.org /2013/04/29/177986761/from-dissections-to-depositions -poets-second-jobs.

Phillips, Robert. "Poets' Work, Poets' Jobs." About.com. Adapted from "How Poets & Writers Earn a Living," *Writer's Chronicle*, December 1997. http://poetry.about.com/od/poetryhistory/a /poetswork.htm.

Pinsky, Robert. "Poetry & Education: Robert Pinsky on the Future of Poetry." Interview by Joyce Wilson. *The Poetry Porch* 1, no. 3. (April 7, 1997). http://www.poetryporch.com/pinsky.html.

Plourde, Marc. "On Translating Miron." In *The Insecurity of Art: Essays on Poetics*, edited by Ken Norris and Peter Van Toorn. Montreal: Vehicule Press, 1982.

Pratt, E.J. "Poet E.J. Pratt on Turning 75." CBC Radio, February 4, 1958. CBC Digital Archives. http://www.cbc.ca/archives /categories/arts-entertainment/poetry/poetry-general /poet-ned-pratt-on-turning-75.html.

Queyras, Sina. "More Lives of Poets." *Harriet* (blog). The Poetry Foundation, March 2010. http://www.poetryfoundation.org /harriet/2010/03/morelives-of-the-poets/?woo.

Reyes, Barbara Jane. "Some Thoughts on Teaching Poetry to Spoken Word Artists." Poets.org, April 15, 2014. http://www.poets.org /poetsorg/onteaching/some-thoughts-teaching-poetry -spoken-word-artists.

Reynolds, Christie Ann. "On Memorization: Some Thoughts on 'Owning' Your Own Work." *THEThe Poetry Blog*, March 16, 2010. http://www.thethepoetry.com/2010/03/on-memorization -some-thoughts-on-%E2%80%9Cowning%E2%80%9D-your -own-work/.

Rose, Rachel. "Poetry Doesn't Care: An Interview with Rachel Rose." By Melissa Bull. *Lemon Hound*, February 20, 2013. http:// lemonhound.com/2013/02/20/poetry-doesnt-care-an-inter- view-with-rachel-rose/.

Ruefle, Mary. *Madness, Rack, and Honey: Collected Lectures*. Seattle: Wave Books, 2012.

Rusche, Harry, ed. "The Poet Speaks of Art." Readings for English 205 "Introduction to Poetry" course, Emory University. http:// english.emory.edu/classes/paintings&poems/preface.html.

Saint-Andre, Peter. "The Individualism of the Poet-Musician." *Monadnock Review*, May 1997.

Sawyer-Lauçanno, Christopher. *E. E. Cummings: A Biography*. Naperville, IL: Sourcebooks, 2004.

Seferis, George. "From A Poet's Journal." In *The Poet's Work: 29 Masters of 20th Century Poetry on the Origins and Practice of their Art*, edited by Reginald Gibbons. Boston: Houghton Mifflin, 1979.

Silverstein, Shel. "One Inch Tall." In *Where the Sidewalk Ends: The Poems and Drawings of Shel Silverstein*. New York: Harper & Row, 1974.

Skelton, Robin. *The Practice of Poetry*. London: Heinemann Educational Books, 1971.

Snyder, Gary. "The Real Work (excerpts from an interview)." In *The Poet's Work: 29 Masters of 20th Century Poetry on the Origins and Practice of their Art*, edited by Reginald Gibbons. Boston: Houghton Mifflin, 1979.

Strand, Mark. "Mark Strand, The Art of Poetry No. 77." Interview by Wallace Shawn. *The Paris Review* 148 (Fall 1998). http://www.theparisreview.org/interviews/1070/the-art-of-poetry-no-77-mark-strand.

———. "The Uncontrollable Elements: An Interview with Mark Strand." By Jean Nordhaus. *Poetry Quarterly* 10, no. 4 (Fall 2009). First published 1991 by the Writer's Center *Carousel*.

Sullivan, Rosemary. *Shadow Maker: The Life of Gwendolyn MacEwen*. Toronto: HarperCollins, 1995.

Teicher, Craig. "What Poetry Reviews Are For (and Up Against)." *Publishers Weekly*, March 29, 2010. http://www.publishersweekly.com/pw/by-topic/industry-news/publishing-and-marketing/article/42613-what-poetry-reviews-are-for-and-up-against.html.

Temple, Emily. "The 30 Harshest Author-on-Author Insults in History." *Flavorwire*, January 1, 2012. http://flavorwire.com/188138/the-30-harshest-author-on-author-insults-in-history/5.

Tinguely, Vincent. "Volunteer Radio Showcases Spoken Word: 'Because Freedom of Speech is Way Too Dangerous.'" *The Canadian Review of Literature in Performance* 4 (2012). http://www.litlive.ca/story/423.

Tranter, John. "The Poetry Kit Interviews John Tranter." The Poetry Kit. http://www.poetrykit.org/iv98/tranter.htm.

Whitman, Walt. "Song of the Open Road." In *Leaves of Grass*. New York: Signet Classics, 2000.

Wright, C. D. "on poetics, collaboration, American prisoners, and Frank Stanford." Interview by Kent Johnson. *Jacket* 15 (December 2001). http://jacketmagazine.com/15/cdwright-iv.html.

Young, James O., and Susan Haley. "Nothing Comes from Nowhere: Reflections on Cultural Appropriation as the Representation of Other Cultures." In *The Ethics of Cultural Appropriation*, edited by James O. Young and Conrad Brunk, 268-89. Malden, MA: Wiley-Blackwell, 2009.

Zomparelli, Daniel. "Poetry is Dead: What the Hell Happened?" *Poetry is Dead* 1 (January 18, 2010). http://www.poetryisdead.ca/content/poetry-dead-what-hell-happened.html.

Zwicky, Jan. "The Ethics of the Negative Review." *Canadian Women in the Literary Arts*, May 18, 2012. http://cwila.com/ethics-negative-review-jan-zwicky/. First published 2003 by *The Malahat Review*.

# Bios

DOUGLAS BARBOUR, poet, critic, and professor emeritus of English at the University of Alberta, has published many books of criticism and poetry, including *Fragmenting Body etc.*; *Lyric/Anti-lyric: Essays on Contemporary Poetry*; *Breath Takes*; *A Flame on the Spanish Stairs*; *Continuations* and *Continuations 2*, with Sheila E. Murphy; and *Recording Dates*. He has read his poetry and lectured in many places around the world, and also performed with Stephen Scobie in the sound poetry duo Re: Sounding. He was inaugurated into the City of Edmonton Cultural Hall of Fame in 2003. He writes a review blog on SF&F and contemporary poetry: https://eclecticruckus .wordpress.com/.

KIMMY BEACH's fifth book, *The Last Temptation of Bond*, was long-listed for the Alberta Readers' Choice Award, was chosen as one of the top five poetry books of the year on *Quill & Quire*'s Readers' Poll and was featured on CBC Radio One's *The Next Chapter* with Shelagh Rogers. She lives in Red Deer, AB.

GREGORY BETTS is the author of five books of poetry and the recent monograph *Avant-Garde Canadian Literature: The Early Manifestations*. He is currently the Director of Canadian Studies and an associate professor at Brock University.

JOE BLADES lives in Fredericton, NB. He is a visual artist–writer, educator, producer-host of the *Ashes, Paper & Beans* at CHSR 97.9 FM, founding publisher of Broken Jaw Press and a past president of the League of Canadian Poets. Blades is the editor of ten collections, and the author of seven poetry books, three of which have also been published in Serbian editions.

YVONNE BLOMER was born in Zimbabwe and came to Canada when she was two years old. Her first collection *a broken mirror, fallen leaf* was shortlisted for the Gerald Lampert Memorial Award. Yvonne has also published two chapbooks, *Landscapes and Home: Ghazals* and *Bicycle Brand Journey*, and is the co-editor of *Poems from Planet Earth* out of the Planet Earth Poetry reading series, of which she is the artistic director. In 2014, her third full collection of poems, *As if a Raven*, was released with Palimpsest Press.

DENNIS E. BOLEN has an M.F.A. in creative writing and taught for two years at the University of British Columbia. He worked as editor for *subTERRAIN* magazine, part-time editorial writer for the *Vancouver Sun* and freelance literature critic for several publications while publishing seven books of fiction. His first book of poetry, *Black Liquor*, was issued by Caitlin Press in September 2013.

KATE BRAID has written and co-edited eleven books of poetry and non-fiction about subjects from Emily Carr to mine workers. She has published five books of prize-winning poetry, most recently, *Turning Left to the Ladies*. Her most recent book of non-fiction is a memoir, *Journeywoman: Swinging a Hammer in a Man's World*.

STEPHEN BROCKWELL is an Ottawa poet who runs a small IT consulting company from a tiny office in the former CBC studios of the Fairmont Château Laurier. His fifth book, *Complete Surprising Fragments of Improbable Books*, was published by Mansfield Press in 2013.

RON CHARACH is the author of nine books of poetry and the collection *Cowboys & Bleeding Hearts: Essays on Violence, Health and Identity*. His letters on a number of topics, especially gun control, appear regularly in the *Toronto Star*, the *National Post*, *The Globe and Mail*, as well as many other Canadian and American newspapers. He recently completed a yet-unpublished novel about the world's gun madness, called "cabana the big." He lives and practices psychiatry in Toronto.

WAYDE COMPTON writes poetry, fiction and non-fiction. His most recent book, *The Outer Harbour*, a collection of short stories, was published by Arsenal Pulp Press in fall 2014. He is the program director of creative writing at Simon Fraser University's Continuing Studies department.

ADAM DICKINSON is a writer, researcher and teacher. His poetry has been nominated for the Governor General's Literary Award and twice for the Trillium Book Award for Poetry. He teaches poetics and creative writing at Brock University in St. Catharines, ON.

S. R. DUNCAN is a producer, publicist, freelance writer and poet. He was long-time owner of Pink Flamingo Works, a graphic design and small press publishing house specializing in literary chapbooks and promotional material for limited budgets. His broadcasting credits include CKNW, CITR, Shaw TV, CJSF and Co-op Radio, where he produced a weekly half-hour radio show called *Wax Poetic* for twelve years. Duncan has blazed a unique trail for himself as a Vancouver arts community builder and a mentor to dozens of artists and small non-profits.

TRISIA EDDY was born, and raised, in Edmonton, and has no plans to leave. Her written work has made its way into a variety of literary journals and collaborations, including the chapbook *Edith & Aurelia: A Romantic Tragedy in Five Acts*, published in 2011 by Chicago's Dancing Girl Press. Trisia has most recently been focusing on letterpress and book arts, and has exhibited both locally and internationally.

JANNIE EDWARDS has published three collections of poetry: *The Possibilities of Thirst; Blood Opera: The Raven Tango Poems* (adapted for the stage and performed at Workshop West's Canoe Theatre Festival); and *Falling Blues* (shortlisted for the Writers Guild of Alberta's poetry prize). Her videopoem *Engrams: Reach and Seize Memory* features a poetic translation of Edwards' English poems into American Sign Language. She has collaborated with a videographer and visual artist on *adrift*, a video and poetry installation; and with performance artists at Edmonton's festival of women in the arts, the SkirtsAfire herArts Festival. She is a founding member of the Mill Woods Artists Collective and an organizer of the collective's monthly Glass Door Coffee House reading series.

GARY GEDDES has written and edited more than forty-five books of poetry, fiction, drama, non-fiction, criticism, translation and anthologies, and won a dozen national and international literary awards, including the Commonwealth Poetry Prize (Americas Region), the Lieutenant Governor's Award for Literary Excellence and the Gabriela Mistral Prize from the government of Chile. His non-fiction books are *Sailing Home: A Journey Through Time, Place and Memory*; *Kingdom of Ten Thousand Things: An Impossible Journey from Kabul to Chiapas* and *Drink the Bitter Root: A Writer's Search for Justice and Redemption in Africa*. His most recent book of selected poems is *What Does A House Want?*, published by Red Hen Press and praised by former US poet laureate Billy Collins.

CHRIS GILPIN is a writer and arts educator originally from Edmonton, AB. His chapbook, *Faux Reals*, was published in 2007 by Full Court Press. In 2013, he became the executive director of Vancouver Poetry House.

SUSAN GLICKMAN works as a freelance editor, primarily of academic books, and teaches creative writing at Ryerson University and the University of Toronto. She is the author of six collections of poetry from Signal Editions of Véhicule Press, most recently *The Smooth Yarrow*; two novels, *The Violin Lover* and *The Tale-Teller*; the Lunch Bunch trilogy of children's books and *The Picturesque and the Sublime: A Poetics of the Canadian Landscape*.

KIM GOLDBERG's *Red Zone* collection of poems about homelessness has been taught in university literature courses. Her previous

collection, *Ride Backwards on Dragon*, was a finalist for the Gerald
Lampert Memorial Award. She is a winner of the CZP/Rannu Fund
Award for Writers of Speculative Literature and other distinctions.
Her non-fiction book, *Refugium: Wi-Fi Exiles and the Coming Electro-
plague*, about electrosensitivity and electropollution, will be released
in 2015. Kim lives in Nanaimo, BC, and online at https://pigsquash.
wordpress.com/.

GARRY GOTTFRIEDSON is from Kamloops, BC. He is a self-
employed rancher from the Secwepemc Nation. Gottfriedson is
strongly rooted in his cultural teachings. He is currently the prin-
cipal at the Sk'elep School of Excellence in Kamloops. He holds
a master's degree in education. In 1987, the Naropa Institute in
Boulder, CO, awarded him a creative writing scholarship. There,
he studied under Allen Ginsberg, Marianne Faithfull and others.
Gottfriedson has eight published books. He has read from his work
across Canada, the United States, Europe and Asia. His work has
been anthologized and published nationally and internationally.

CATHERINE GRAHAM is the author of five collections of poetry,
including *Her Red Hair Rises with the Wings of Insects*, a finalist for the
Raymond Souster Award. Winner of the IFOA's Poetry NOW: 6th An-
nual Battle of the Bards and an Excellence in Teaching Award, she
teaches at the University of Toronto's School of Continuing Studies.

HEATHER HALEY pushes boundaries by creatively integrating
disciplines, genres and media. Her writing has been published in
many journals and anthologies and she is the author of poetry
collections *Sideways* and *Three Blocks West of Wonderland* and the

novel *The Town Slut's Daughter*. Haley has directed numerous video-poems, official selections at dozens of international film festivals, and toured Canada, the US and Europe in support of two critically acclaimed AURAL Heather CDs of spoken word songs, *Princess Nut* and *Surfing Season*.

BEATRIZ HAUSNER's recent poetry books include *Sew Him Up* and *Enter the Raccoon*. *La Couturière et l'homme-poupée*, a French translation by Patricia Godbout and Héloïse Duhaime has just been published by Les Éditions de la Grenouillère. Hausner has translated many poets of Spanish American surrealism, including César Moro and Mandrágora.

STEVEN HEIGHTON's most recent books are the *The Dead Are More Visible, Workbook: Memos & Dispatches on Writing* and *Every Lost Country*. His 2005 novel, *Afterlands*, appeared in six countries, was a *New York Times Book Review* editors' choice and was a best of year choice in ten publications in Canada, the USA and the UK. His short fiction and poetry have received four gold National Magazine Awards and have appeared in *London Review of Books, Best English Stories, Best American Poetry, Zoetrope, Tin House, Poetry, Brick, The Literary Review, New England Review* and five editions of *Best Canadian Stories*. Heighton has been nominated for the Governor General's Literary Award and Britain's W. H. Smith Literary Award, and he is a fiction reviewer for the *New York Times Book Review*.

BARBARA HUNT is a poet, fiction, non-fiction and screenwriter who has been published in literary journals, anthologies and magazines across North America including CBC Radio One and *Homemakers*

magazine. She was selected for a Diaspora Dialogues poetry mentor-
ship in Toronto and published her first poetry book, *The Patternmaker's
Crumpled Plan*. As well as her writing work with Phanta Media in
Markham, writing communities like The Writers' Community of
Durham Region and Ontario Writers' Conference are her heart.

AMANDA JERNIGAN is the author of two books of poetry,
*Groundwork* and *All the Daylight Hours*, and a short prose book, *Living
in the Orchard: The Poetry of Peter Sanger*. She edited *The Essential
Richard Outram* for Porcupine's Quill, and is currently at work on
a scholarly edition of Outram's poems. She lives in Hamilton, ON,
with her family.

BRUCE KAUFFMAN lives in Kingston, ON, and is a poet, writer,
editor and workshop facilitator. His publishing history includes a
chapbook of poetry, *seed*, and a stand-alone poem, "streets." Three
full collections of his poetry launched in 2013: *The Texture of Days,
in Leaf and Ash; a seed within* and *The Silence Before the Whisper Comes*.
He currently hosts a monthly open mic reading series (poetry @ the
artel), a weekly spoken word radio show on CFRC 101.9 FM in Kings-
ton (*finding a voice*) and facilitates 'intuitive writing' workshops.

M. TRAVIS LANE lives in Fredericton, NB, and has published four-
teen books of poetry, the most recent: *The Crisp Day Closing on my
Hand*, *The Book of Widows*, *The All Nighter's Radio* and *Ash Steps*. An
interview between Anita Lahey and M. Travis Lane was published
in issue 180 of *The Malahat Review*. A fifteenth collection, *Crossover*,
will appear in 2015.

CHRISTINE LECLERC is one of six editors of the Enpipe Line project, in which about a hundred people go dream versus dream with the Northern Gateway Pipelines project. Jen Currin, Jordan Hall, Ray Hsu and Nikki Reimer are other collaborators.

TAYLOR LEEDAHL has published two works of poetry, *No Apologies for the Weather* and *Hybrid Hibiscus*. In 2013, she received her M.A. in art history from Concordia University for her thesis on interspecies collaborations in contemporary art. Leedahl currently lives in Saskatoon where she works in the arts and as an assistant in an entomology lab.

SHAWNA LEMAY is an Edmonton writer. Her latest book is *Asking*.

CHRISTINE LOWTHER is a lifelong activist and resident of Clayoquot Sound since 1992. She is the author of three books of poetry, co-editor of two collections of essays and appears in *Force Field: 77 Women Poets of British Columbia*. Her memoir, *Born Out of This*, was released in fall 2014 by Caitlin Press.

JEFFREY MACKIE is a Montreal poet and literary journalist. Mackie has had his poetry published nationally and internationally and has been translated in Croatia. An engaging poetry performer, videos of his readings can be found on YouTube. Mackie also has a regular literary feature on the *Tuesday Morning After* radio show on CKUT 90.3 FM. In 2012, he ran for the Green Party in the Quebec provincial election and he plays in the Montreal Hockey League of the Arts.

KATH MacLEAN is a multimedia artist and educator living in Edmonton. Her most recent work is *Kat Among the Tigers*, poetry based on the journals and correspondence of Katherine Mansfield, and its accompanying poetryvideo, *Doo-Da-Doo-Da*, which won her the "Best of Fest" at its first national and international screening. Inspired by the writing of Robert Kroetsch, MacLean's poetry was short-listed for the Robert Kroetsch Award for Innovative Poetry in 2012, the same year she received the inaugural Anne Green Award for her excellence and innovation in film, poetry and performance. In 2013, she was writer-in-residence at the Mackie Lake House for Kalamalka Press, and, in 2015, she will be writer-in-residence at the Al Purdy House in Ontario.

ALICE MAJOR has published nine collections of poetry and a book of essays (*Intersecting Sets: A Poet Looks at Science*). She won the Pat Lowther Memorial Award for *The Office Tower Tales* and served as Edmonton's first poet laureate (writing poems about hockey and potholes). She is founder of the Edmonton Poetry Festival and a recent recipient of the Writers Guild of Alberta's Golden Pen Award.

MARK McCAWLEY is the founder, publisher and in-house editor of Greensleeve Editions, which publishes the online magazine of transgressive art, writing and music, *Urban Graffiti*. He is the author of ten chapbooks of poetry and short fiction, most recently, *Sick Lazy Fuck* and *Just Another Asshole: Short Stories* from Greensleeve Editions. His short fiction has also appeared in the anthologies: *Burning Ambitions: The Anthology of Short-Shorts*, edited by Debbie James and *Grunt & Groan: The New Fiction Anthology of Work and Sex*, edited by Matthew Firth and Max Maccari. Most recently his work has appeared in *The Toronto Quarterly, Sensitive Skin* magazine and the *Evergreen Review.*

Born in Ottawa, ROB MCLENNAN is the author of nearly thirty trade books of poetry, fiction and non-fiction. He won the John Newlove Poetry Award in 2010, the Council for the Arts in Ottawa Mid-Career Artist Award in 2014 and was long-listed for the CBC Poetry Prize in 2012. His most recent titles include *Notes and Dispatches: Essays* and *The Uncertainty Principle: Stories,* as well as the poetry collection *If suppose we are a fragment.* An editor and publisher, he runs above/ground press, Chaudiere Books, *The Garneau Review* (ottawater.com/garneaureview), *seventeen seconds: a journal of poetry and poetics* (ottawater.com/seventeenseconds), *Touch the Donkey* (touchthedonkey.blogspot.ca) and the Ottawa poetry PDF annual *ottawater* (ottawater.com). He spent the 2007–8 academic year in Edmonton as writer-in-residence at the University of Alberta, and regularly posts reviews, essays, interviews and other notices at robmclennan.blogspot.ca.

A graduate of Simon Fraser University's The Writer's Studio, JANE MELLOR was host and organizer of The Writer's Studio Reading Series, a monthly literary event for notable and emerging authors. Her poetry has been published in *Quills Canadian Poetry Magazine, emerge,* The Writer's Studio website, *The Toronto Quarterly,* Leaf Press's *Monday's Poem* blog, *Contemporary Horizon Magazine, Contemporary Horizon Anthology, Poetry Nook* and *The Maynard,* and her poem "The Day The Rain Stopped" was long-listed in the UK's National Poetry Competition out of over twelve thousand entries. *Delicate Availability* is Mellor's first book of poetry and prose.

GARRY THOMAS MORSE's books include the first novel in his Chaos! Quincunx series, ReLit finalist *Minor Episodes / Major Ruckus*, and *Discovery Passages*, finalist for the Governor General's Literary Award and the Dorothy Livesay Poetry Prize. Morse now recluses in Regina, SK.

WENDY MORTON has six books of poetry, and a memoir, *Six Impossible Things Before Breakfast: Taking Poetry Public Across Canada*, in which her adventures as a corporately sponsored poet are revealed. She has been WestJet's Poet of the Skies and Chrysler's Poet of the Road. She is currently sponsored by AbeBooks. She is the founder of Canada's Random Acts of Poetry. She is the recipient of the 2010 Spirit Bear Award, the Sheri-D Wilson Golden Beret Award and was made an honorary citizen of Victoria in 2011 for her contributions to the arts. In 2012 she was awarded The Colleen Thibaudeau Outstanding Contribution Award from the League of Canadian Poets. She has, for the past four years, been working with school districts in British Columbia on The Elder Project, getting young adults to interview their elders and write poems, mostly in First Nations communities.

BONNIE NISH is founder and executive director of Pandora's Collective Outreach Society, a charitable organization in the literary arts based in Vancouver, BC. She is also executive producer of the Summer Dreams Literary Arts Festival, an outdoor annual festival. Bonnie has a master's in arts education from Simon Fraser University and is currently pursuing a Ph.D. in expressive arts therapy at the European Graduate School. Published widely in such places as the *Danforth Review* and the *Ottawa Arts Review*, Bonnie's first book of poetry, *Love and Bones*, was launched into the world in September 2013 by Karma Press.

STEVE NOYES has published six collections of poetry; his most recent is *Small Data*. His second novel, *November's Radio*, will be published by Oolichan Books in fall 2015. He lives in Victoria.

PATRICK M. PILARSKI is the author of *Huge Blue* and two chapbooks. His work has appeared in journals and anthologies across North America, Europe, Australia and Japan, including *The Fiddlehead*, *PRISM international* and *The New Quarterly*. Patrick is co-editor of *DailyHaiku*, an international journal of contemporary English-language haiku, and has served as vice president for The League of Canadian Poets. He lives in Edmonton, AB, with his wife and fellow writer, Nicole Pakan.

ROBERT PRIEST is the author of fourteen books of poetry, three plays, two novels, seven musical CDs, one hit song and many columns for *NOW Magazine*. *Rosa Rose*, a book of children's verse in praise of inspirational figures, recently won a silver Moonbeam Children's Book Award in the US. His latest book of poems for adults is *Previously Feared Darkness*.

ANGELA RAWLINGS' first book, *Wide slumber for lepidopterists*, transitioned to the stage in 2014 through the efforts of composer Valgeir Sigurðsson, record label Bedroom Community and VaVaVoom Theatre. Rawlings received a Chalmers Arts Fellowship (2009–10). She was the 2012 Queensland Poet-in-Residence, creating the in-

206/ The Other 23 & a Half Hours

terdisciplinary ecopoethics project *Gibber*. In 2013, her work *Áfall / Trauma* was short-listed for the Leslie Scalapino Award for Innovative Women Playwrights. Rawlings recently launched *Figure*, an online poetry oracle (with Sachiko Murakami). Her librettos *Longitude* (with Davíð Brynjar Franzson, Davyde Wachell and Halldór Arnar Úlfarsson) and *Bodiless* (with Gabrielle Herbst) debuted in 2014.

HAROLD RHENISCH writes poetry, poetic non-fiction and fiction-non-fiction grafts from his home in Vernon, BC. He prunes trees and poems, too, for friends, publishers and writers, and is currently writing about two things he loves: Iceland, and the strong links between the American Civil War and the peaches of the Okanagan. He has published twenty-seven books, including *Motherstone: British Columbia's Volcanic Plateau* and *The Spoken World*, poems he wrote with Robin Skelton, five years after Robin went to spirit.

RACHEL ROSE is a Canadian-American poet, essayist and short story writer. She has published three collections of poetry, *Giving My Body to Science*, *Notes on Arrival and Departure* and *Song and Spectacle*.

JOE ROSENBLATT was born in Toronto in 1933. Rosenblatt has written more than twenty books of poetry, several autobiographical works and his poems have appeared in over thirty anthologies of Canadian poetry over his forty-year career as a poet. His poetry books have received major awards, such as the Governor General's Literary Award for poetry in 1976 and the BC Book Prize in 1986. His most recent book, *Dark Fish & Other Infernos*, published fall 2011, is a collaborative work, a savagely satirical epistolary exchange with Catherine Owen.

STUART ROSS is the author of about fifteen books of fiction, poetry and rant, most recently the collaborative poetry collection *Our Days in Vaudeville*. He runs the micropress Proper Tales, has his own imprint at Mansfield Press and is a founding member of the Meet the Presses collective. He lives in Cobourg, ON, and blogs at bloggamooga.blogspot.ca.

Eco-science poet and interdisciplinary adventurer MARI-LOU ROWLEY has encountered a timber wolf, come between a black bear and her cub, interviewed an Italian astronaut, found over forty-four four-leaf clovers and published nine collections of poetry. Her most recent books are *Unus Mundus* and *Transforium* in collaboration with visual artist Tammy Lu. Her work has appeared internationally in literary, arts and science-related journals including the *Journal of Humanistic Mathematics* (US) and *Aesthetica* magazine's Creative Works competition (UK).

JAY RUZESKY teaches English, creative writing and film studies at Vancouver Island University. His latest book is *In Antarctica: An Amundsen Pilgrimage*.

SANDY SHREVE's fifth poetry collection, *Waiting for the Albatross*, is forthcoming in spring 2015. Her previous books include *Suddenly, So Much* and the anthology *In Fine Form: The Canadian Book of Form Poetry* (co-edited with Kate Braid in 2005). She edited *Working For A Living*, a collection of poems and stories by women about their work and founded BC's Poetry in Transit program. Her work is widely anthologized and has won or been short-listed for a variety of awards. She lives on Pender Island, BC.

GLEN SORESTAD is a well-known Canadian poet who lives in Saskatoon. His poems have appeared in literary magazines all over North America and other countries; they have been translated and published in seven languages. His poems have appeared in over sixty anthologies and textbooks, as well as in his more than twenty books and chapbooks of poems published over the years.

PAUL VERMEERSCH is the author of several poetry collections, including the Trillium Award–nominated *The Reinvention of the Human Hand* and *Don't Let It End Like This Tell Them I Said Something*. Vermeersch holds an M.F.A. in creative writing from the University of Guelph for which he received the Governor General's Gold Academic Medal. His poems have been translated into Polish, German and French and have appeared in international anthologies. He has taught creative writing at the University of Guelph and Sheridan College, and currently teaches creative writing at the University of Toronto's School of Continuing Studies. He was, from 2001 to 2012, the poetry editor for Insomniac Press, and he is now senior editor for Wolsak & Wynn Publishers, Ltd. He lives in Toronto.

PATRICIA YOUNG has received numerous awards for her poetry. Her most recent book is *Summertime Swamp-Love*.

CATHERINE OWEN lives in New Westminster, BC. She is the author of ten collections of poetry, among them *Designated Mourner* (ECW Press, 2014), *Trobairitz* (Anvil Press, 2012), *Seeing Lessons* (Wolsak & Wynn, 2010) and *Frenzy* (Anvil Press, 2009). Her poems and memoirs are included in several recent anthologies, such as *Force Field: 77 Women Poets of British Columbia* (Mother Tongue Publishing, 2013) and *This Place a Stranger: Canadian Women Travelling Alone* (Caitlin Press, 2015). Her collection of memoirs and essays is called *Catalysts: Confrontations with the muse* (Wolsak & Wynn, 2012).

    *Frenzy* won the Alberta Book Prize and other collections have been nominated for the BC Book Prize, the ReLit Award, the CBC Prize and the George Ryga Award. She works in film and TV, plays metal bass and blogs at *Marrow Reviews* on WordPress.com.